MW00436802

An English Manual

For the Elementary School

Dorothy Harrer

Printed with support from the Waldorf Curriculum Fund

Published by:
The Association of Waldorf Schools
of North America
3911 Bannister Road
Fair Oaks, CA 95628

Title:	*An English Manual* *For the Elementary School*
Author:	Dorothy Harrer
Design, Layout and Cover:	Hallie Jean Wootan
Editor:	Hallie Jean Wootan
Proofreader and Copy Editor:	Charles H. Blatchford

First printed by Mercury Press in 1985
Second Printing 1990
Third Printing 1996
Fourth Printing 1998
Revised, reedited edition by AWSNA 2004

Contents

Excerpts from *Practical Advice to Teachers* by Rudolf Steiner

On Language Teaching[1]

Rudolf Steiner emphasizes *"word teaching" (parts of speech) under twelve years of age and syntax after twelve. Sentence structure can be given when the parts of speech have become familiar. The right approach to developing understanding of sentences is to draw the child into making statements about what is going on around him. An understanding of what subject and predicate do can come about through the difference between an impersonal sentence such as*—It is raining—*which arises from our intimate relation with the world, and a sentence with a subject such as*—The grass grows green—*in which, by making a subject, we have detached ourselves more from the world. He makes the point that in merely stating an activity, as in the first example, we are bound up in that activity.* [Lecture 9]

This involvement becomes clearer in what he has to say about the inner activity that accompanies the use of verbs, nouns and adjectives. [Lecture 4]

---

[1] The author cited passages from an earlier and undetermined edition of Rudolf Steiner's *Practical Advice to Teachers: Fourteen Lectures* (Great Barrington, MA: Anthroposophic Press, 2000.) These lectures, given in 1919 and popularly known as "The Practical Course," are currently available.

In her earlier version of this work, the author cited page numbers which are now not useful as the quotations themselves cannot be found in the current version of Steiner, possibly due to retranslation. Because of incongruities and indeterminate or useless references, quotation marks and page references have been omitted in this reprint version, and material which is believed to come from Steiner, but unverifiable word for word, is italicized.

In this edition of *An English Manual*, pedagogical rationale of Steiner is italicized without quotation marks and a reference is made to a particular lecture where you, dear reader, may find the totality of Steiner's thought on the particular subject. It might be noted that with regard to language, Steiner was referring to foreign languages in general, and not specifically English.

—Editor, Fair Oaks, May, 2004

Verbs

When I use a verb, "Someone writes," I not only associate myself with the individual of whom I use the verb, but I participate in the action of his physical body, I perform it with him . . . but merely as tendency.

Nouns

Through all that is expressed in nouns we become conscious of our independence as human beings. We disassociate ourselves from the outer world in learning to describe things by nouns.

Adjectives

It is quite another matter when we describe things by adjectives. When I say, "The chair is blue," *I define some quality which unites me with the chair.*

Vowels and Consonants [Lecture 2]

We shall only learn to understand speech if we see it as fundamentally anchored in human feeling. Speech is the expression of conflicting sympathetic and antipathetic activities in the breath system, accompanied by the activity of the brain. When we combine a vowel with a consonant, we always combine sympathy and antipathy. Our tongue, our lips and our palate are really intended solely to function as antipathy-organs, to ward things off. Vowels must be sought as human shades of feeling, consonants as imitations of external things.

Feelings expressed in Vowel Sounds

oh   amazement, astonishment or fear

ah   wonder

ay   resistance

ee   indicating, approaching

How to Use Examples

In grammatical teaching the examples must be dropped and in no sense carefully entered into notebooks, but the rules must remain.

Method

Derive a rule from examples you have invented, then a day or so later return to the rule and let the children invent examples for it; or let them show how the rule applies to some thing they have memorized in a poem or some other passage. [Lecture 9]

Composition

Composition in the elementary school should be the recounting of incidents which have occurred, of experiences, and not free composition. This leads to accurate observation in later life. [Lecture 10]

Teach language so as to:

1. *engage the whole individual*

2. *bring him to a selfless relationship with the external world.*

Writing, Spelling, and Reading

It is important that reading never be done with the mere eye, but that the activity of the eye passes over into the entire activity of the human limbs. The children then feel, unconsciously, right down into their legs, what they would otherwise survey only with the eye. [Lecture 1]

Writing is, in a sense, more living than reading. Reading isolates man from the world. When writing is developed from an origins image behind the form of a letter, the abstract character of writing is overcome. In writing we have not yet ceased to imitate world-forms, as long as we derive it from drawing. [Lecture 9]

Grammar and Syntax

When we elevate unconscious speech into the knowledge of grammar, we pass with our pupils from unconscious language to the higher plane of a fully conscious approach.

Unconsciously, or half-consciously, in fact, man climbs in life up to the external world in a way corresponding to what he learns in grammar. [Lecture 4]

Literature

Storytelling

If you convey your own mood when you tell stories, you will tell them so that the child relives with all his body what has been told. We must have the feeling that we are moving the whole child, and that only from the emotions we excite must the understanding for the story come. [Lecture 2]

We guide the child to educated speech by telling him stories, and letting him retell them, and correcting the mistakes he makes. [Lecture 12]

Poetry

It is of extreme importance to draw the child's attention in every poem to the music underlying it.

Detailed explanation of poems, verging perilously on grammar, is the death of all that should influence the child.

There must flow in from the rest of the teaching what is necessary for the understanding of the poem. [Lecture 3]

Reading

That which has been assimilated only by understanding the meaning, only affects the observation the thought perception—but the will is not educated. The will likes to sleep with does not wish to be fully awakened— by the perpetual unchaste laying bare of the meaning. The will cannot be forced by simply throwing light on the meaning.

With the child we must study subjects which do not lay bare the meaning. Then we shall educate his will. . . . For the thinking we must definitely practice subjects concerned with revealing meanings.

Composition

In the elementary school we should practice recounting of experiences that have occurred, for the child must learn this art of reporting. Otherwise he will not be able to play his proper role in human social life.

Then there will be inculcated in the child the habit of inventing nothing in life or in a court of law, but to relate the truth of external facts. [Lecture 10]

Special Topics from the Waldorf Curriculum

The use of the "conditional" sentence in the 6th grade in speaking and writing is a means of developing a strong feeling for style.

In the 7th grade the teacher should develop a "truly plastic perception" through speech of the expression of desire, wonder, surprise, etc. The child should learn to form sentences out of the inner character of these feelings.

Notes from a Composition Workshop Among Teachers

When we look into the original curriculum, we find assignments that call upon us as teachers to visualize and form abilities in the children out of their inner capacities at their various ages.

In the first two grades, no task is set that involves the children in either introspection or sense impressions directly obtainable from nature. All writing assignments come out of what he has been told in class (supposedly in imaginative pictorial presentations).

Only in the third grade is it suggested that they begin to call upon what they have experienced through sense impressions and through their own feelings.

After the connection between their moral feeling and practical life has been prepared in the third grade, composition of all kinds of letters, even little business letters, leads them in the fourth grade into ways of relating themselves to others through what they write.

Fifth grade work in composition seems to be an expansion of ways of expressing the differences between what the children do, and what happens to them (active and passive attitudes). What *they* think can be compared with what they get from some other person as that person's opinion or words (as in direct quotation).

Sixth graders must be drawn into the conditions that affect life, by learning to understand and express the ways in which they, or others, are judged or diverted by outer circumstances that have an important bearing on their own life experiences.

In the seventh grade writing that expresses wish, wonder, and surprise is a bridge between the inner feelings, the dawning of self-concern, and the lawful and guided world of nature and human destiny.

Business compositions, or exercises in practical communications, or expressions of practical matters, continue from the fourth grade up to give the children a vicarious of experience how to deal with others in matters that do and can affect them.

It would seem that the work in composition writing must be guided by an effort on the part of the teacher to help the children, through their own verbal skills to approach and deal with the world into which they are emerging.

Composition in elementary school should be recounting of incidents that have occurred, and not free composition. "Incidents that have occurred" hints at the healthfulness of objectivity. The child who recounts the story of a trip or vacation with a rather dull and methodical inventory of events is on more secure ground than one who writes about an imaginary companion who disappears like "a pat of butter on a hot pan."

Placing children squarely in their own experience is like giving them ground to stand on.

If the teacher speaks from his own experience, telling a story from out of his own life, a class can be inspired to do likewise, first contributing via the spoken word in class, then writing their stories down, at home.

The teacher can go further and help children to understand how to create various moods in their writing. One way would be to read examples from literature wherein the mood is one of curiosity, or of wonder (awe), of sympathy (compassion), or of gladness and joy.

One can refer to a writer's notebooks, wherein he makes accurate records for later use.

Vocabulary can grow not so much in the direction of knowing the meaning of more and more words, but in the appreciation for what words can do:

- make pictures: *torn, jagged, lacey, pale, steep*
- give sound sensations: *creak, whack, crunch, bellow, thump"*
- give sensations of how things feel when touched: *rough, squashy, slimy, silky, velvety, prickly*
- sound like what happens: *pump, dig, slop, splinter, hit, scratch, scrap*
- embody inner feeling: *merry, mournful, lonely, alert, cheery, gloomy*

Through such words the objective relationship to the surrounding world can be strengthened.

Second Grade

The Four Kinds of Words

One spring day a little gnome woke up a little seed-child who was sleeping soundly underground.

"Wake up, wake up!" cried the gnome.

And the little seed-child answered, still half asleep, "Oh, oh, I have been asleep so long that it is hard to remember who I am! Please, kind gnome, tell me my name."

"I remember your name," answered the gnome, "for I have to remember the names of all the seed-children. Last autumn you gave me your name to keep for you, and now you may have it back. It is Violet."

As soon as she had heard her name from the gnome, the little violet-child felt happy and really wanted to wake up and do something.

"Now what shall I do?" she cried.

"My friend, the water fairy, will tell you that," answered the gnome.

So he called the water sprite who spoke to the little violet and said, "You must *grow*!"

As soon as the violet heard the word *grow*, she pushed her little head up; and stretched her little feet down. She pushed and stretched, while the gnome danced around singing her name, "Violet, Violet!" and the water sprite brought her many cool drinks of water, saying, "Grow, grow."

Then the gnome and the water sprite held hands and danced together and sang together, "Violet grows, Violet grows."

Just as the little violet's head peeped above the ground into the air, an air fairy greeted her saying, "Fast ! Violet, grow fast."

Now the gnome, the water fairy and the air fairy were all singing together, "Violet grows fast!" And she did. Her little green stem grew tall, her little green leaves grew broad, and her little head grew larger and larger.

Then, one day, a sun fairy came to the violet and touched her head with his wand of light, saying, "I bring you a color from the rainbow, and it is purple."

The violet felt so happy that she lifted her head up, opened her eyes wide and let forth her beautiful purple petals; while now the gnome, the water fairy, the air fairy and the sun fairy all sang to greet her with the words each one had given:

"The purple violet grows fast."

The gnome had given her a name, the water fairy had told her what to do, the air fairy had told her how to do it, and the sun fairy had dressed her in a color from the rainbow.

We can call these four kinds of fairy words *name* words, *doing* words, *how* words and *color* words.

The following day the children can be called upon to retell and act out the story of the little violet and the four fairies.

We use name words, doing words, how words and color words all the time when we speak or write. We can also find them in what we read. Here is a little story on the board. Let us read it together and then look for the four kinds of words in the story. We will color all the name words blue, the doing words red, the how words orange and the color words green.

The yellow sun shone brightly.
The green buds opened slowly.
The blue bird sang sweetly.
The red fox ran fast.
The brown rabbit jumped high.

Doing Words—An Introduction to Verbs

On the blackboard a picture has been drawn of a child who stands erect between the earth and the sky. On one side of him in the green grass there grows a plant. On the other side an animal moves on four feet, with head down.

The children are asked to stand, straight and tall, like the child in the picture. They say, in chorus, "I *stand.*" *Stand* is then written below the feet of the child in the picture. To the question, "What else can you do with your feet?" one *walks*, another *jumps*, another *runs*. Soon the words, *walk, run, jump, skip, hop, dance* are written below the feet of the child in the picture.

Then comes the question, "What can you do with your hands?" The answers come and are written near the hands of the child in the picture: *draw, write, paint, knit, crochet, clap, give, hold.*

"What can you do with your eyes, your ears, your nose, your mouth, your voice?" And the answers written about the head of the child in the picture: *see, look, hear, listen, smell, taste, eat, chew, speak, sing.*

"Who does all these things?" The answer: "I." And *I* is written over the head of the child in the picture.

Now it is time for the children in the class to draw such a picture themselves and to copy the words that express what each can do.

The following day the transition can be made from reading the picture to writing simple sentences:

I stand.	I knit.	I smell.
I run.	I speak.	I taste.
I write.	I look.	and so forth

The capital "I" and the period at the end can be explained and practiced.

Now the children read what they have written.

The next question arises: "What do we say when not *I* but someone else does some of these things?" The word *I* can become someone else's name. A child is asked to do something and another is asked to tell what he did.

Kate hops.
John writes.
Ann speaks.
and so forth

In writing these expressions down, it is discovered that an *s* is added to the word that tells what each one does.

Finally the teacher comes to the point of explaining that the words that tell what someone does are called "doing words."

In the picture there are a plant and an animal. A third lesson can start with the question: "What can the plant do?" The answers then can be written down as sentences, beginning with capital letters and ending with periods.

The plant grows.
The bud swells.
The flower blooms.
The seeds form.

"And what can the animal do?"

The animal runs.
The animal eats.
The animal barks, squeaks, roars.

"What can the human being do that the animal cannot do?"

The human being writes, draws, paints, knits, speaks, sings, reads. These human actions can be written out in simple sentences for the children to copy into their notebooks. Further examples can be developed and the children allowed to find and underline the doing words:

I <u>stand</u>.	The lamb <u>eats</u> grass.
The <u>lamb</u>	The wolf <u>eats</u> meat.
The wolf <u>runs</u>.	Mary <u>sings</u> a song.
John <u>sings</u>.	Ann <u>knits</u> a scarf.
The lamb <u>bleats</u>.	A mouse <u>eats</u> cheese.
The wolf <u>growls</u>.	The cat <u>chases</u> a mouse.
Tom <u>talks</u>.	A dog <u>chases</u> the cat.

Name Words and Doing Words

A recitation occurs first and is followed by a writing lesson. All the names can be written in blue, the actions in red. The use of capital letters and periods is important.

Frogs jump.
Caterpillars hump.
Worms wiggle.
Bugs jiggle.
Rabbits hop.
Horses clop.
Snakes slide.
Seagulls glide.
Mice creep.
Deer leap.
Foxes prowl.
Dogs growl.
Puppies bounce.
Kittens pounce.
Lions stalk.
I walk.
　　　—author unknown

The following verses were adapted from *The Golden Treasury of Poetry*, edited by Louis Untermeyer.

A fish swims. A bone bleaches.
A bird flies. A stone sinks.
A horse runs. A cat screeches.
A partridge struts. A rat blinks.
Flint sparks. A mole creeps.
A lily blooms. A coal burns.
The oven glows. A frog sleeps.
A tiger roars. A dog learns.

Picture words are added to describe the name words.

A wet fish swims. A dry bone bleaches.
A live bird flies. A dead stone sinks.
A strong horse runs. A scared cat screeches.
A plump partridge struts. A poor rat blinks.
Hard flint sparks. A soft mole creeps.
A white lily blooms. A black coal burns.
A hot oven glows. A cold frog sleeps.
A savage tiger roars. A good dog learns.

Emphasis on picture words.

A wet fish—a dry bone—
A live bird—a dead stone—
A strong horse—a scared cat—
A plump partridge—a poor rat—
Hard flint—a soft mole—
A white lily—a black coal—
A hot oven—a cold frog—
A savage tiger—a good dog—

These verses can at first be taught as recitation. Once the children know them, they can become writing lessons in which the Name Words, Doing Words, and Picture Words are looked for and perhaps underlined, or written in blue (names), red (doing words), and green (picturing words).

Third Grade

Name Words and Doing Words

The children have started their main lesson on Bible Stories and have heard the story of Adam and Eve. Now in connection with English, we go back to this story, and the teacher reads them from *Genesis*, Chapter 2:

> And the Lord God said, It is not good that man should be alone.
>
> And out of the ground the Lord God formed every beast of the field, and every fowl of the air, and brought them unto Adam to see what he would call them; and whatsoever Adam called every living creature, that was the name thereof.
>
> And Adam gave names to all cattle and to the fowl of the air, and to every beast of the field.

We can imagine Adam in the beautiful Garden of Eden. God's light shone in the Garden among the trees and the flowers, and God's voice spoke, creating and bringing the animals before Adam that he might name them.

There were the cattle, the cows, the bulls, the sheep, and the goats which grazed on the grasses while mooing and bleating.

There were the wild beasts—roaring lions and tigers and panthers which crouched and leaped and ran.

There were the climbing and creeping creatures—squirrels, wood-mice, lizards, snakes, snails and earthworms.

There were the flying creatures, birds of all sorts and insects; and the swimming creatures, the fishes and the whales.

And as they appeared, walking, running, leaping, hopping. creeping, flying, and swimming, Adam named them all.

Now we are going to act this out. Each one of you think of an animal and of something the animal does, so that you can act it out. Eric will be Adam, and as each animal comes by him, he is to name it and say what it is doing.

(As the children act, the teacher writes the name words and the doing words on the board, in the following short sentences:

The fish swims.	The deer runs.
The bird flies.	The tiger roars.
The squirrel climbs.	The sheep bleats.
The snail creeps.	The fox barks.
The cow grazes.	The bird sings.
The lion leaps.	The owl hoots.

The children copy the sentences that they have developed, writing the names in blue and the actions in red.)

Review (the following day)

Yesterday, Adam named all the animals and we wrote their names and what each did in short sentences. Today you may each have a turn to name someone or something and tell what he, she. or it does in a sentence.

Now I am going to give you a riddle and ask you to find the answer:

"Born with one name and given another, one like, one unlike the name of my brother. What are my names?"

(The children try to guess the answer, but probably fail.)

I will tell you the answer to this riddle. Every person has a special name which is the same for everyone; yet each one can only call himself by that name; he cannot call anyone else by it. That is the name we are each born with. What is the name we call ourselves? "I." We each can say "I" about ourselves, but we have to call others by the names their fathers and mothers gave them, and these names are not usually alike.

Now, whether you write down your given name, or the name "I," you must always begin the name with a capital letter. And if you will turn to the pages of sentences you wrote yesterday, you will see that the first word in each sentence is a capital letter. Let us read the sentences we wrote yesterday.

What do you find in every sentence, besides a capital letter at the beginning and a period at the end? A *name* word and a *doing* word. Every sentence, no matter how short or how long, must have a name word and a doing word in it.

In what I shall now write on the board, I want you to find the sentences. Whenever one sentence ends, we will put in a period, and then begin the new sentence with a capital letter. Then you will see how the meaning become clear.

The paper tore the little girl cried sadly the poor boy tripped the girl laughed loudly a hot fire burned the cat purred happily the sharp knife cut the man called the dog ran fast.

Picture Words

Do you all remember the story of "The Fisherman and His Wife?" (The story can be retold, with a blackboard picture of the sea, which changes its color as the story progresses.)

Now, you see, the more the fisherman's wife asked for, the more angry the sea became, and its color changed from blue to dull green to violet. Then it became dark grey, then black. All these changing colors paint pictures of the way the sea looked to the fisherman. We can call these words—*blue, green, violet, grey, black*—picture words. They all describe the sea. Now there are many kinds of picture words that can describe people and things.

Let us paint some pictures with picture *words* (and not paint a real picture.) We will use a color, though, for the picture words—green. The name words will be blue, the doing words red. As I write these short sentences on the board, I want you to think of a picture word that will describe the name in the sentence.

The _white_ stone cracked.   The _green_ grass grew.

The _pink_ flower bloomed.   The _brown_ cow mooed.

The _brave_ lion roared.   The _fat_ pig grunted.

The _thin_ man ran.   The _yellow_ leaves fell.

The _yellow_ sun shone.   The _little_ boys played.

The _wild_ wind blew.   The _lazy_ girl slept.

The _grey_ rain fell.   The _bright_ stars twinkled.

How? Words

Children, I would like to ask you which is better: to write an assignment quickly and carelessly, or slowly and carefully? How you *do* your lessons is as important as *what* you do. There are many ways in which you can do something. Let us act them out.

I speak *quietly*.

I speak *loudly*.

I clap *softly*.

I tramp *heavily*.

I smile *sweetly*.

I scowl *fiercely*.

I move *slowly*.

I skip *happily*.

(Different children can be called upon to act out the above sentences.)

What does the last word in each of these sentences tell us? It answers the question, *How*? We can call these words "how" words.

Look at these three sentences on the board:

The wind blew.

The wild wind blew.

The wild wind blew loudly.

Which sentence tells us the most? The last one, in which there is not only a name word and a doing word, but also a picture word and a how word. This last sentence is also the most interesting.

In these blanks add a picture word and a how word:

The _____ boy walked _____.

The _____ man ran _____.

The _____ fire blazed _____.

The _____ cow chewed her cud _____.

Now we have learned about four different kinds of words that can be used to describe something. Of these four, the name word and the doing word are the most important in a sentence, and the picture word and the how word make each sentence more interesting.

A Third Grade Lesson on Adverbs

Review "how" words

Introduction to words that tell when, where or how.

The old man limped painfully.	(How?)
The old man turned back.	(Where?)
The old man arrived late.	(When?)

John came quickly.	(How?)
John finished first.	(When?)
John went away.	(Where?)

Mary stood near.	(Where?)
She listened well.	(How?)
She left early.	(When?)

The plump cow chewed her cud contentedly.
The cow wandered far and near.
The lazy cow reached the barn last.

We came in.
They went out.
The tallest boy walked in front.
The little boy walked before.

List words that answer

How?	When?	Where?
painfully	late	back
quickly	first	away
well	early	near
contentedly	last	far
bravely	now	in
honestly	later	out
wisely	sometime	behind
foolishly	never	before
falsely	immediately	here
cruelly	forever	there
softly	then	somewhere
loudly		around
		up
		down
		in front

Subjects for Composition

Choice of One

A Story about My Pet

My Dolls

A Wild Animal I have Watched

When My Wish Came True

The Worst Storm in My Life

The Things I Like to Do in Summer

A Dream I Remember

My Favorite Place

Lost, and Found Again

If I Had Three Wishes

What I would Like to Be

Verses for the Four Sentences

Commands

> Listen to the night wind blow.
> See the swirling flakes of snow.
> Close the window. Shut the door.
> Keep out the wild wind's angry roar.
> Light the fire. Let it blaze.
> Warm the house with its hot rays.

Exclamations

> How wonderful the morning is!
> Oh, what a sparkling day!
> Sky's blue around the golden sun!
> The wind has died away!

Statements

> The golden sun shines on the snow.
> The trees blue shadows make.
> The colors of God's own rainbow
> Twinkle in each snowflake.

Questions

> Where do snowflakes come from?
> Why are they so white?
> Who gives them each a separate form?
> How far has been their flight?
> And what creates the rainbow
> In each white star of snow?

> —Dorothy Harrer

Fourth Grade

Thoughts and Deeds

The following story, with its accompanying thoughts and verses, brings the essential qualities of the noun and the verb into the realm of life experience for the fourth graders.

The Four Brothers

Once upon a time there was a great and wise king who ruled over a vast kingdom, and over the course of time he had four sons.

When the day came for the four brothers to leave their father's house and to go in search of kingdoms of their own, they said to their father, the King: "O father, thou art wise and mighty, ruler of a vast kingdom. We who now go forth in search of kingdoms of our own can only further extend thy kingdom. Tell us the secret of your greatness that we may rule wisely and well and be true sons of our father."

Then said the King, "My sons, even as there are four of you, so do I rule my kingdom by the power of four thoughts, and in these four thoughts do I hold sway. In telling them to you, I make you a gift of my wisdom. If these thoughts become your deeds, then will your kingdoms prosper. The choice is yours."

The four brothers remained silent and listened as the King revealed the four most secret thoughts of his mind.

Said the King:

"Four thoughts dwell in my mind; With them my kingdom bind.

The first one is thus sure
That all life must endure.

The second one I know
Is that all life must grow.

The third is yet more real
That all of life must feel.

The fourth is ever so
That all of life must know.

To endure, to grow
To feel, to know,

These thoughts dwell in my mind,
With them my kingdom I do bind."

The four brothers then went out from their father's house, taking with them this gift of wisdom in the words,

To endure, to grow,

To feel, to know

and each brother tried to understand their meaning.

At first the four brothers traveled together. They journeyed far from their father's house down a path that had no turning. At length they reached a place where the road divided into four branches. If there had been only two forks of the road, or five, or six, they would have wondered which to take, but as there were just four, they plainly saw that here they were to part, each one to go his own way.

"Remember the words of our father," they said to each other, "and let his wisdom guide us, that his thoughts may become our deeds, and that in the kingdoms which we find to rule, his kingdom will be extended."

Thereupon they touched each other for the last time, and each one went his own way along one of the four forks in the road.

Now we must remember that the four thoughts of the King had dwelt together in his mind just like four petals of a single flower. So, too, as long as the brothers had traveled together down the single path, these four thoughts had been as one; but now that the four brothers had parted, each one began to wonder which of the four sayings was the best and which one to choose for himself.

One brother, who had turned toward the north, said to himself, "What could be better than for all things to *endure* and to last forever? That is my choice: my kingdom shall endure and last forever. I will make everything so solid and firm that nothing can destroy it."

The second brother said, as he went toward the south, "What could be better than for all things to *grow*? That would mean that they are alive. This is my choice: in my kingdom all things will be alive, ever-growing, ever-changing, and always renewed."

The third brother thought, as he traveled toward the east, "What could be better than for all things to *feel*, to love the good and to hate the bad. This is my choice: that all beings in my kingdom will love what is good for them and hate what is bad for them."

The fourth brother, traveling to the west, did not think as his brothers did. He did not wonder which of his father's thoughts was the best. Rather, he wondered which one would explain the meaning of all the others. He said to himself, "If I, and all who live in my kingdom, could but *know* the meaning of all my father's thoughts, then would his wisdom truly guide us. It must be that, of the four, to *know* is the key to such wisdom. This is my choice."

Thus it was that the four sons of the King established four kingdoms on earth, and the King's thoughts became their deeds.

He, who chose the thought "to endure," built his kingdom with rocks and firm earth. His was the kingdom of wide plains and rolling hills, rocky cliffs, and mountain peaks, the kingdom of earth itself!

He, who chose the thought "to grow," filled his kingdom with growing life, grass, flowers, and trees that sent their roots into the kingdom of earth, and their shoots upward toward the sun. The plants themselves were the second son's kingdom—forever growing, blooming, fading, letting their seeds fall to earth only to grow again.

The brother, who chose the thought "to feel," peopled his kingdom with creatures who were not only alive but who felt hunger and moved busily over the earth in search of food; creatures who felt love and took care of their young; who felt hate for all that endangered their lives and fought for their food and their loved ones. These were the animals and it was their kingdom over which the third brother ruled.

In the kingdom of the fourth brother, who had chosen the thought "to know," lived beings who not only had a share in the other three kingdoms, but who also had a fourth power. They not only had firm bodies, growing bodies, and feelings of love and hunger and hate, but they also had the power to know and to understand the earth, the plants, and the animals.

And so it was, that when the great and wise king learned how wisely his four sons had extended his kingdom over the earth by transforming his thoughts into their deeds, he summoned them into his presence and spoke these verses:

Four deeds on earth can well be found

To endure, to grow,

To feel, to know,

We meet all four the whole world round.

The rocks of earth endure and bear

The weight of foot,

The grip of root,

The wash of waves and windy air.

The plants in earth do grow and wane

As seed and flower

Helped by the power

Of shining sun and splashing rain.

The beasts on earth feel love or hate;

> With fang and paw
> Or beak and claw,

Each kind will fight for food and mate.

And man can know the world's true need

> For rock and tree
> And beast, and he

Can learn to do the four-fold deed.

After returning to the story of the "Four Brothers" on the following day, the teacher raised the question, "What is a deed?" and continued as follows.

In the story of the "Four Brothers," the human kingdom is the one that can know but the King had told his sons, "If my thoughts become your deeds, your kingdoms will prosper." What he meant was that what we learn and think and know, we must also be able to do.

There was once a little boy who thought he knew a lot, although he was very young. He knew that if he crossed the street with the green light, he'd be safe; but he didn't do it. He crossed during the red light, and a car knocked him down. He knew that if he washed his hands before eating, his mother wouldn't send him away from the table, but he didn't do it; and at every meal he had to be told to go back upstairs and wash. He knew that if he'd put his clothes in order at night, he'd find them easily in the morning, but he didn't do it; and too often he was late to school because he had to look for a shoe or a sock.

Here in our class there is someone who knows that the whole class would be happier if he would raise his hand and wait to be called on, but he doesn't do it. There is another who knows that with more care there would be fewer mistakes to correct in her writing, but she does not do it.

This is the meaning of turning thoughts into deeds. It isn't enough to know something. If it is worth knowing, it is worth doing too. We know that a sentence is a whole thought, and that we should put a period at the end of a sentence, but some don't do it. We know that when something new takes place in a story, we should start a new paragraph, but we don't do it. When we learn things in school, it isn't just to have them in mind, but in our will too.

Punctuation Verses

A grammar class is greatly enlivened when the following verses are acted out by the children.

I am the period. I love to rest.
All sentences stop at my request.

I want to know
What is your name?
Where do you live?
What is your fame?
What answer will you give?
The question mark am I,
And can you tell me why?

Whoopee! Hooray!
Look out! Make way!
I'm here ! I'm there! I'm everywhere!
Whatever the excitement rare,
The exclamation point is there!

When the sentences are long,
Running ever on and on,
I run with them, so nimble and merry,
To give you a breathing space,
            lest you grow weary.
I am the comma, so nimble and busy,
Without me some sentences might make you dizzy.

In choosing the pupils to take the parts of these four punctuation marks, it is easy to find a phlegmatic child to dramatize the period, a melancholic for the question mark, a sanguine for the exclamation point and a choleric for the ever-active comma.

Four Kinds of Sentences and the Four Punctuation Sprites

When we want to write a letter
Four kinds of sentences make it better.

The question asks—
Statements reply—
Commands set tasks
Which exclamations defy!
But none of them would be well understood
If four punctuation marks weren't so helpful and good.
These four little sprites make our thinking quite clear.
To tell who they are is why we are here.

The Parts of Speech Verses

Verses by Virginia Field Birdsall

The Verb

I am a verb, I like to act,
To walk, to run, to dance—it's a fact.
To plow, to build, to work, to strive,
I like to feel that I'm alive!
But sometimes I just say, "I am,"
And act as meek as a little lamb.

The Noun

I am a noun; I give names to things,
To persons, from beggars to royal kings;
To animals also, great and small;
To flowers and trees that grow so tall,
To things like tables and chairs and sticks,
To houses and stone, concrete and bricks;
And to things you can't see or hear or feel,

Like goodness and truth and honor and zeal!
I like to be quiet—I don't run about—
I just sit still and let others shout.

The Pronoun

I am a pronoun; it isn't quite fair—
I'm only about when the noun isn't there!
Sometimes I'm "*I*" and sometimes I'm "*you*,"
Or "*he*," "*she*," or "*it*," or "*they*" or "*them*," too;
I change my form when it suits my whim,
Then *she* becomes *her* and *he* becomes *him*.

The Articles

The articles small are we;
We like to make ourselves known:
Fat *A*, *an* and *the*—but not one of us three
Can stand for a minute alone.

Three small articles are we
And we keep nouns company.

The Adjectives

We are the adjectives—artists, too—
We stick to the nouns as your skin sticks to you.
I call the man *great* or *good* or *sad*.
I call the beast *large* or *fierce* or *bad*.
I paint the grass *green* and the flowers *gay*.
We dance through the world in our *colorful* way.

The Adverbs

We are the adverbs! We're lots of fun
Telling *how, when* or *where* the action is done;
Whether *neatly*, or *carelessly*, *promptly* or not,
We have you children right on the spot.
You act *bravely* and *honestly*, *wisely* and *well*,

Or *falsely* and *foolishly*, adverbs will tell.
Either *now* or *later* or *sometime* or *never*,
Immediately, *presently*, *soon* or *forever*,
Either *here* or *there* or *somewhere around*,
Along with the verb the adverb is found.
But sometimes we go with the adjectives, too,
When the sun's *very* bright and the sky's *very* blue.
Or with other adverbs we sometimes mate,
When you walk *very* slowly and come *very* late.

The Preposition

A preposition small am I,
But others are not half so spry!
I'm *up* the mountain, *down* the glen,
Through the city, *among* the men,
Under the river, *over* the sea,
Or up *in* the tree-tops! There you'll find me.
I'm *with* and *of* and *from* and *by*,
Pointing always, low or high.

The Conjunction

I am the word that joins—conjunction:
I have a plain but useful function.
What would you do without your *and*?
Your *or*? Your *if*? I'm in demand,
Because, unless your work you do,
You're negligent and lazy, too!

The Interjection

I'm the interjection wild,
Dear to almost every child.

Oh! how lovely! *Ouch!* take care!
Alas! Hurrah! Hello! Beware!
Oh! how noble! *Look!* red light!
My! you gave me such a fright!

Fourth Grade Lessons

Nouns

The human being can stand erect upon the earth, with legs and feet to support him, while his hands are free to work in many ways. No matter what he may be doing, his head is carried quietly about. If he is running or jumping, the head goes along; if he is swinging a bat, throwing or catching a ball, he does it with his arms and hands while his head stays still. The quiet head! Is it sleeping? Does it ever do anything? Yes, it does! Imagine that your arms and legs are so tired that you just want to sit still and rest. You are sitting very quietly, so quietly that no one even knows that you are around. Yet your quiet head is at work. You *see* a shadow moving across the window. You look more closely and see that it is a bird that has flown to the window sill. You *hear* a wild noise and know that your cat is having a fight with his friends. You *smell* smoke and know that it is an autumn bonfire out in the yard.

You can see, hear, smell, and even taste things with eyes, ears, nose and mouth—all parts of your head; and then you can *know what it is* that you see, hear, smell or taste.

When you know what something is, you *name* it.

Now, sit perfectly still and name something you see or hear or smell or touch.

Can you name something that you can't see, hear, smell, taste or touch?

We have a long list of names on the board. We have learned to call such words "name-words." The grown-up word for a name-word is "noun."

We must learn and remember: A noun is the name of a person, place or thing. It is also the name of an action, a feeling or a thought.

Verbs

If we had to sit still all the time while we looked and listened and gave names to things, nothing much would happen in our lives. No houses would be built, no clothes would be sewed, no bread would be baked, no pictures would be painted, and no music would be played.

Human beings must not only know what lives in the world but they must *do* something with it, or they wouldn't be proper human beings. Without his head, a man couldn't give names to things; without his hands and feet he couldn't do things. He couldn't build or bake, plow, or plant, or paint.

Can you act out something with your hands or feet so that we can guess what kind of action it is?

What else can you do? Think? Plan? Sleep? Hope? Listen? Look? How many things can you do without using your hands and feet? Speak? Sing? Laugh? Cry?

Let us write down some of the actions we have mentioned. These are all *doing* words, action words. Grown-ups call them "verbs."

Just as a human being has to have both head and limbs, so in a whole thought we must name what the thought is about and tell what the thing we named does. Every sentence is a thought, and every sentence must have a noun telling what the sentence is about and a verb to tell what the noun does.

Let us name some things and tell what they do. Let's write the nouns in a quiet blue, the verbs in an active red.

A stone falls.	Grass grows.
The wind blows.	Seeds sprout.
Birds fly.	The boy writes.
Lions roar.	The man speaks.
The girl sings.	Jane sews.

What is the most important verb which must be true before any other verb can be true?

I *am*.	We *are*.
You *are*.	
He *is*.	
She *is*.	They *are*.
It *is*.	

What is a verb? A verb is a word that tells what someone or something does, or is.

Adjectives

A story that can be used to introduce the study of adjectives in fourth grade follows:

"The Judas Tree," from *Jataka Tales*, selected by Francis & Thomas, Cambridge University Press, 1916.

Once upon a time a king had four sons. One day they sent for the King's charioteer and said to him, "We want to see a Judas Tree; show us one."

"Very well, I will," the charioteer replied; but he did not show it to them all together.

First he took the oldest son to the forest and showed him the tree when it had no leaves as yet.

When the leaves had sprouted and were green, he took the second son to see it.

He took the third son to see it when the pink blossoms were out.

And the fourth son was shown it when it bore red fruit.

One day after this, when the four brothers were sitting together, someone asked, "What sort of a tree is the Judas Tree?"

The first brother answered, "It is brown, like a dead stump."

The second brother cried, "It is green like a banyan tree!"

The third, "No, it is pink like the clouds at dawn."

And the fourth said, "It is red like a piece of meat."

Then the four brothers became angry at each other's answers and ran to find their father.

"My lord," they each asked, "what sort of a tree is the Judas Tree?"

"What is that you say?" asked the King.

Then they told him their various answers.

Said the King, "All four of you have seen the tree. Only, when the charioteer showed you the tree, you did not ask him, 'What is the tree like at such a time, or at another time?' You never thought of that, and that is the reason for your mistake."

Then the King repeated a verse:

"All have seen the Judas Tree

What is your perplexity?

No one asked the charioteer

What is its form the live-long year!"

In our story each son pictured the Judas Tree in a different color: brown, green, pink, and red. These picture words gave color to the tree. So it is that certain words give color to other words: they paint pictures as if they were artists.

Can you find words to give color to the things or animals in these sentences?

The _____ stone sinks.

The _____ bird sings.

The _____ lion roars.

The _____ grass grows.

The picture words, *gray, blue, golden, and green* tell us something more about the nouns. Any words that tell us something more about nouns are called "adjectives." Adjectives can give the nouns color, shape or feeling: as, *yellow, round, and sad.*

What we must remember: An adjective is a word used to describe a noun.

Adverbs

If someone said, "The thin man spoke," we might ask the following questions:

How did he speak? (*poorly? well? clearly? vaguely?*)

When did he speak? (*first? last? early? late?*)

Where did he speak? (*here? there?*)

Then we could ask, "How well?" (*Very well!*) Or, "How thin?" (*Extremely thin!*)

The *extremely* thin man spoke *there first* and *very well.*

All these italicized words answer the questions, How? When? and Where?

There, first and *well* tell us where, when and how he spoke. These words tell us something more about his action in speaking. They go with the verb *spoke*. Words that go with, or describe, a verb are called "adverbs." But we can also see that these adverbs also describe other parts of speech: *extremely* describes *thin*, an adjective; and *very* describes *well*, another adverb.

(Now let the children discover the adverbs in other examples, underlining them and drawing arrows from them to the words they describe, as below.)

A <u>very</u> small, <u>terribly</u> thin child stood <u>quietly</u> in

the street. It was snowing <u>heavily</u>. <u>Very</u> few

passersby noticed her. Some who came <u>near</u> <u>enough</u>

saw her <u>partly</u> torn coat and <u>badly</u> worn shoes and that

she was trying <u>bravely</u> not to cry.

A rule to remember is that adverbs describe verbs, adjectives, and other adverbs. Adverbs answer the questions how, when, and where.

The Preposition Game

Some small object, in our class a miniature seal, can be hidden somewhere in the classroom, while one child is out of the room. When he comes in, he has to find out where "Sammy Seal" is hiding, by asking if he is:

in the wastebasket
under a table
behind a book
on the window sill
near the lockers
beside a chalk box
among the plants, and so forth

After several children have had turns finding Sammy Seal's hiding place by means of such questions, the phrases used are written on the blackboard. Then the question can be asked, "Which words in these phrases show the *position* where Sammy might be hidden?" The answers are prompt and correct: *in, under, behind, on, near, beside, among,* etc.

As these words that seem to point out a position come before the other words in the phrases, they are called *prepositions.* (The syllable "pre" is found in other words we know that express the idea of *before,* such as prehistoric, prepare, prefer, precede.)

Each preposition points to some object that is named. This is the noun in the phrase, and it is called the object of the preposition. The phrase, as a whole, is called a "prepositional phrase."

Vowels and Consonants

We are going to go back to what we learned in the first grade when we learned the alphabet. It is good to remember how we learned about the letters because we are now going to learn something more about them in a more grown-up way.

We learned many of the letters from pictures, for such letters grow out of pictures of things to be found in the outside world.

Butterfly

Fish

King

Mountain

Wave

Tree

Snake

Valley

We learned to call the sounds of these letters "whisper sounds"; for when we sound these letters we find that they whisper. Try to sound out each of the above letters alone: B, F, W, M, T, S, V.

The grown-up words for these whisper sounds we must now learn to use. These letters are *consonants*. All the letters in the alphabet, except for five, are consonants.

The five letters which are not consonants are the ones we called "singing sounds" in the first grade. We learned them as sounds that we make to express our own feelings:

When we feel wonder as we look at the beautiful sunset or rainbow, we say, "Ah!"

When we see a little baby, or a little kitten, that we want to love and hug, we say "Oh!"

If a cold wind blows so that our bones ache and we turn blue, we say, "Ooo-oo!!"

When we feel excited and point to something that suddenly shows up, for instance a mouse under a chair, we say "Eee-ee!!"

Then there is the sound "Ay," which makes us feel ourselves. It often means the same as the word "Yes," Or the word "forever." It is a very positive sound.

And you probably remember "I" (Ah-ee), the name we each say when we speak of ourselves. This sound lives inside us more than any other sound.

These sounds come from the letters: A E I O U. When we speak these sounds, they are not whispers, but they sing out clearly and carry the voice out into the air. That is why we called them singing sounds in the first grade. The grown-up word for them is vowels.

Every word we speak or write or read is made up of vowels and consonants. In the vowels we are close to our feelings; in the consonants we are close to the outside world.

Some words show this more than others, and so they are

squirm	chatter	tickle	whirl	whistle	whisper
wiggle	shiver	scratch	whir	rustle	
squeak		itch		bustle	
		twitch			

dark	thick	fuss	flow	roar	rumble
star	quick	flame	fly	bellow	
mumble					
	lick	flap	flip	shout	
murmur					
breathe		trip	wrinkle	catch	growl
choke		slip	shrink	flash	prowl
strangle		flip	wink	smash	dig
dangle					dip

When we learn spelling rules, we really see and hear how the vowels and consonants sound when they work together. They don't always sound alike.

Sometimes a vowel is long—ate; sometimes short—at.

A consonant may be hard—cake; or soft—ice;

crust; city;

rag; rage.

A consonant may be light—hiss; or heavy—his;

And sometimes the consonants are there, but are silent— know write sign walk climb . . . . .

In order to know about the world we live in, we have to be able to understand words: the words we hear, the words we read, and the words we have to write. We have to spell out the vowels and consonants in all these words. There is a certain magic in letters and sounds—in words, as such. A long time ago people thought that words had magic powers, because they believed that God's word had given them life. And people believed that every word they uttered was an offering back to God.

Now when we practice spelling, let us remember the connection between the following words: spell (meaning "magic" spell); Gospel (God's word) meaning God's spell!

An Introduction to the Tenses of Verbs

Time doesn't wait for anyone!

How do we use our time?

Every morning we wake up. We have been sound asleep, and we don't know what's been going on while we were asleep. Maybe it has rained. The leaves and blossoms and grass have been coming out while we slept. When we wake up we look forward to the day, and remember yesterday. Often, in remembering, we realize that we have forgotten something! Not because we wanted to, but because something happened to make us think and do something else rather than what we should have done. We have forgotten to take home paper and pen, or pencil. We have forgotten to put our assignment down. Or we have remembered, and we come to school, through a nighttime of sleep, ready with our work, mysteriously remembering what we heard in our classes the day before, and looking forward to what will follow on the coming day.

Every moment of life is a meeting point of past, present, and future time.

I have been planting seeds. They were formed in the past. Now they are put into the ground to lie in the earth, and I know they will sprout in two or three weeks. They will grow, will bring forth leaves, then blossoms, then seed-pods or fruit containing new seeds which will, in the future, bring forth new plants.

Everything we learn today comes out of yesterday and will help us to grow into the future.

Much depends on what we do at present; the present time always becomes the past, and the past is important for the future.

What we have done, or left undone, in the present, becomes the ground on which we stand for the future.

The present moment comes from somewhere, like a river that flows down from a mountain height, and it is moving toward the ocean of life in the future.

Past, Present, and Future

The class, having had at least part of their study of Norse Myths, can hear again the story of Yggdrasil and the Three Norns, leading thus to a consideration of the three tenses.

Yggdrasil, the great ash tree, extended its roots into three different worlds: the world of life, the world of death and the world of the wisdom of Mimir who was wise because he remembered all that had ever happened.

Nidhogg, the serpent, gnawed at the root that extended into Niflheim, trying to kill the tree. He was opposed by the three Norns who daily watered the root with the water of life so that the tree would never die.

These three sisters were white-haired Urd, who was concerned with the Past; Verdandi, concerned with the Present; and Skuld, the veiled sister, whose concern was the Future. The three Norns continually knitted threads together, each thread being the life of a single human being. Now and then a thread would be cut and some man' s life would end. A new thread would soon take its place and a new life on earth would begin to take its place among other lives.

Every day the gods would travel in a happy company to visit the three sisters and learn of the Past, the Present, and the Future. It was on one such visit that Odin learned that one day the Fenris wolf would devour him

You children are very young, but you are old enough to have memories of when you were even younger! One of my memories is of being chased by a rooster when I was only two years old. I remember the rooster and that I ran as fast as I could. What do you remember? (Let the children call upon their memories.)

Right now you are in school doing something. What are you doing, Melinda? Are you taking a sour-ball out of your desk?

Tomorrow our vacation starts. What will you do in the next two weeks? (Let the children tell some of their plans.)

In the following lesson three short written assignments can be worked through, starting with:

1. "I remember—"
2. "I am—" or "We are—"
3. "I shall—"

Fifth Grade

The Game "Four Questions"

Someone, as "it," leaves the room.

The class chooses some object in the room.

"It" comes back and has to find out what the object is by asking questions that can only be answered by "Yes" or "No." These questions must make use of adjectives, verbs, adverbs, and finally nouns.

For example:

Is it red?
Is it large?
Is it round?
Is it heavy?

Does it tick?
Does it roll?
Does it hang?
Does it swing?

Does it move?
Does it move easily?
Does it move fast?

Is it the door?
Is it the fan?
Is it a desk lid?

Active and Passive Verbs

It makes quite a difference whether you say: "Victor was scolded by his mother" or "Victor scolded his mother." The first statement sounds more likely.

Again, it is such a different matter if Barbara pokes John, than if Barbara is poked by John. Everyone in the class knows what happens when it is John who has been attacked, who has himself "done nothing, nothing at all!" And when it is the other way around, and it is Barbara who has done nothing—well,

"Barbara is poked by John," very soon changes to "Barbara pokes John."

In the first sentence, Barbara receives the poke; in the second she gives it.

When you take partners to go to the park for recess, it makes a difference whether you choose your partner, or are chosen as a partner. For instance, if Tommy chose Jill, he would probably be feeling very friendly; but if Tommy were chosen by Jill or any girl, it is likely that he might try to walk on the other side of the street!

We begin to see that the subject of a sentence can be either active or acted upon. In the following sentences, underline the verbs, in red if the subject is active, in blue if the subject is acted upon.

The lion ate the man.
The lion was eaten by the man.
The cat scratched the lady.
The cat was scratched by the lady.
The dog wagged his tail.
The dog was wagged by his tail.

In each of these sentences the meaning is changed, quite a bit, depending on whether the subject is giving or receiving the action expressed by the verb. The meaning is actually changed by a change in the verb. To keep the meaning the same, we have to change the subject to go with the change in the verb.

The horse pulled the cart.
The cart was pulled by the horse.

In the following sentences, the subject either acts or receives the action. Change each one to its opposite without changing the meaning.

Billy caught the ball.
Jack ate the apple.
Betty opened the window.
The wind blew the leaves.
The race was won by the fastest runner.
The key to the cupboard was lost by the lady.
The train was stopped by the brakeman.

We have learned that verbs are action words, but in the sentences: I am, You are, He is,—where is the action? Just "to be" is a state of stillness, and when any form of the verb "to be" is connected with an active verb, it becomes inactive or *passive*.

Thus it is that when the subject of a sentence acts, we call the verb an active verb. When the subject receives the action, then the verb is passive. We can say that the verbs speak in either an *active voice* or a *passive voice*.

(This introduction to the voice of a verb can lead to conjugating verbs in all three simple tenses in both active and passive voice.)

The Rule

When the subject in the sentence acts, we say the verb is active. If the subject is acted upon, then the verb is passive.

Find the active and passive verbs in the following verses.

Seven men rode seven horses
All around the track.
Seven men went seven miles
Before they all came back.

Seven horses were ridden
Around by seven men.
Seven miles were traveled
Ere they were back again.

Prepositional Phrases

The children can be called upon to act out given phrases:

(Stand) behind your chair.
(Walk) around your chair.
(Sit) on your chair.

(Go) to the door,
into the hall.
(Knock) on the door.
(Come) into the room.
(Sit) on your desk, under your desk,
at your desk.

What question do all these phrases answer? "Where?"

Then a story, told only in phrases, can be developed, each child contributing a phrase. It might develop like this:

through the door
to the street
on the bus
across town
at the store
on Broadway
down the block
to my house, etc.

These phrases still answer the question "Where?"

Can you think of any phrases that answer the question "When?"

at sunrise
after breakfast
before school
during the morning
about noon
in the afternoon
at four o'clock, etc.

Are there phrases that answer "How something is done?"

(He moved) with ease
(She walked) with difficulty
(She looked) in surprise
(It lives) in fear, etc.

What part of speech answers the questions How? When? and Where? The adverb. So it is that the prepositional phrases that answer these questions are doing the work of adverbs and are called *adverbial* phrases.

A written assignment should follow wherein each child writes a story in prepositional phrases that answer the questions How? When? and Where? Through this experience they feel strongly the need for the complete sentence, and they can then be asked to use such phrases in sentences that tell the complete story.

I went through the door, to the street, and got on the bus. I rode across town, stopped at a store on Broadway, then went down the block to my house.

Now they can be asked to find the prepositional phrases in sentences such as:

The man (in the black coat) rang the doorbell (of the yellow house). The door (of the house) was green. A dog (in the house) began to bark. A dog (on the street) also barked. A policeman (on duty) came by and stopped. A window (on the second floor) was opened. An old lady (with white hair) looked out and called, "There's no one here!"

The man (in the black coat)
The doorbell (of the yellow house)
The door (of the house)
A dog (in the house)
A dog (on the street)
A policeman (on duty)
A window (on the second floor)
An old lady (with white hair)

These phrases all answer the same question, Which?—which man? which doorbell? which dog? which policeman? which window? which old lady?

What part of speech answers the question Which? The adjective. Phrases that do the work of adjectives are called adjective phrases.

Adverbial phrases and adjective phrases do the same work in a sentence as do adverbs and adjectives. The adverbial phrases modify the verbs, and the adjective phrases modify the nouns.

A Way to Interest Fifth Graders in the Way to Form Paragraphs

Compare different people and you will find at least four kinds.

I.

There is the kind who chatters about anything or everything all at once.

> "I was out yesterday in the rain storm and got soaked to the skin. Look at that woman getting on the bus. Now I have a cold. I haven't had a cold for six months. Oh dear! My stocking has a run in it. The leg of the dining room table is broken and I received a splinter. What do you do for colds?"

II.

Then there is the kind of person who never seems to get ahead with what he is saying. He keeps repeating something he has already said.

> "I went to see my cousin who lives out on Long Island. I went out to Long Island to see her. She lives in a nice, new house. The house is very nice and new with a flower garden in front of it. We picked a large bunch of flowers from the flower garden in front of the house."

III.

Then we know people who never enjoy life very much, even though they see things clearly and remember them well.

"In the room there were three tables and many chairs. The room had four windows and four doors. There were some lamps on the tables There was also a piano."

IV.

The fourth kind of person is always knocking into something. He is most alive when he can act and react. He doesn't easily stand off from what is going on. Such a pupil once wrote his teacher the following report.

"The fight started like this. Philip purposely knocked over David's lunch box. When Spencer picked it up, Philip hit him. I tried to break it up, so Philip attacked me. It developed into a fight. Spencer tried to break it up, but Tommy attacked both of us. That is when you came in."

Questions leading to discussion of these four paragraphs:

- Which one is the most clear and interesting?
- Which one has a real beginning and a good ending?
- Which one is most confused or mixed up?
- Which is boring?
- Which one is like a list of objects without color or feeling?

The teacher could then as sign the first paragraph to the sanguine children, the second to the phlegmatics, the third to the melancholics, and the fourth to the cholerics, with the task in each case to rewrite them so as to improve on them. In the effort the children need a little guidance.

- In paragraph I, leave out what doesn't belong,
- Write paragraph II without repeating anything that's been said before.
- Rewrite paragraph III so as to create a fuller picture of the room.

- In paragraph IV, find a way to explain how the fight could have been avoided.

Sixth Grade

The Sense for Speech

Speaking, writing, reading, and thinking are powers which distinguish human beings from animals. Speaking to one another and understanding the speech of others—the sense for speech—is as much one of our senses as seeing or hearing. This sense for speech belongs only to the human being. No animal has it to the same degree.

Many creatures are silent and have no voice: the butterfly, ant, snail, worm, spider. Other creatures make sounds, but the sounds arise from their legs or wings: the bumblebee's wings, the cricket's legs; flies, mosquitoes, katydids. These insect sounds express no feeling, but go on and on in a monotonous way, always repeating themselves, no one sounding any different from any other. None of these creatures have warm, red blood. As soon as you listen to the sounds of animals which have warm, red blood, then you will hear that they have voices which express feeling. Yet these animal voices are capable of expressing only the immediate feeling of such an animal—hunger, pain, fear, or pleasure. An animal cannot separate its noises from its feelings. A cat cannot purr when it feels angry; it needs must growl. A dog cannot keep from howling if it feels pain or loneliness. A robin has a certain song in the springtime which is never heard in the fall. If you listen to animal sounds of all kinds, you will notice this more and more: the shrill cackle of a hen announcing that she has laid an egg; the bleating of a lamb who feels lonely; the hungry screaming of baby birds as the mother bird arrives with an insect or worm for them; the calling of a mother cat to her kittens when she feels that they are wandering too far afield.

The human being can express his feelings too. Before a baby learns to talk, his cries, his laughs, and his whimpers are expressions of how he feels. Mothers can even recognize which cry is one of anger, or of hunger, or of pain. As a human being grows up, however, he learns to talk and to understand speech and then he becomes able to explain why he feels happy or sad. He can even keep still and not say a word, no matter what he feels.

Can you imagine any animal being able to explain how to make something, to describe a beautiful landscape, to tell a story of adventure? An animal can do none of these things, but a human being can.

Now I will read you three different passages. Afterwards I want you to tell me how they are different.

The Paper Wheel

There is a curious little toy that a boy might amuse himself by fashioning in a leisure hour. Some thin cardboard, one or two sheets of common notepaper and a bottle of white glue are all the materials that are required. The spokes and tire of the wheel must be made of cardboard. The wings or sails must be cut from thin paper and made triangular in shape. One side of the triangle must be fastened to one spoke in such a way as to leave the wing curved after the manner of a sail filled with wind. Toss the wheel into the air and move a fan rapidly under it. It will mount into the air, revolving as it sails about.

In front of the house stretched one of those pleasant, sloping cow pastures along French Creek, with a row of trees looking down from the brow of the hill and at the bottom the water rippling over its flat shale bed on its way from one quiet pool to another. A rail fence wandered down to the water's edge, and a great oak and a gnarled cherry tree stood halfway down the slope as if they had started toward the creek and could not decide to go forward or back.

Mike Fink and Henry found Old Al. Old Al saw them coming. When they reached the river bottom, Old Al raised his tail. He hit Mike Fink and Henry on the tops of their heads and rammed them down into the mud. He rammed them down so far that the bottom of the river was half a mile over their heads.

With such examples, the teacher can draw from the children their recognition of the difference between an explanation, a description, and a story in which the action is of first importance. This lesson can be followed with written exercises, or short compositions, in which the children are asked to write on topics such as the following:

An explanation	How to play a game.
	How to make something.
	How to find the common denominator of two fractions.
	How to find the way from school to your house.
A description	Of something you have seen.
	Of someone you know.
	Of something you have listened to.
A narrative	Stories of true adventures in your own experience.

The children can be led to recognize that nouns are the important words in an explanation, adjectives in a description, and verbs in a narrative.

Conditional Sentences

"The use of the conditional sentence in the sixth grade, in speaking and writing, is a means of developing a strong feeling for style."—from Stockmar's *Curriculum*.

The work began with written assignments, as follows:

1. Write about something that happened to you, or to someone you know, because of an unexpected event. Then write what might have happened if this chance event had not occurred.

2. You have plans for a coming weekend, or a vacation. However something might happen to upset your plans. Were this to happen, what kind of weekend would you have instead?

3. Describe the conditions under which you live at the present time. Then imagine and write what you think your life would be like were these conditions removed or changed.

4. Put yourself in another's place, from the point of view of giving him some helpful advice, and write what you would do if you were he.

5. Imagine some uncertain situation, maybe in a court case or a mysterious situation. Is the witness telling the truth? Is the accused giving a true alibi?

The way we live is influenced by all sorts of conditions. Our plans for the future are often altered by unexpected, yet decisive, events. As we grow older and have more to look back upon in a life, we discover the coalitions which caused us to follow a particular path through life.

There is a variety of conditions that play their part in our lives. To express this variety we have to understand it.

1. There are those conditions which are the *cause* for what happened.

    Because he missed the plane, his life was spared.

    As she had good ideas, she was given the job.

    Because of their wartime service, my parents met.

    Because they were married, I was born.

2. There are conditions under which certain things will be done, or are possible.

    If all goes well, I should spend the weekend at the sea shore. Should I still have a cold, I would have to stay home.

    Unless something unforeseen occurs, I shall be there by noon.

    If I am delayed, I shall phone you.

    Provided he has finished his school work, John will come with me.

3. We can compare expressions of *cause* and of *condition*.

    As I live in midtown Manhattan, I have nowhere to play except on the street.

    If I lived on a farm, I could run through the fields.

    Because of electric power, skyscrapers can be practical.

Were the power to fail, the elevators would be useless.

4. Conditions that are *contrary to fact* can be imagined and expressed.

> If I were you, I would be careful
>
> What would you do if you were I?
>
> If he knew the answer, he would tell you.
>
> Had she gone, she would have enjoyed the play.

5. One can also express conditions which *may* or *may not* be true.

> If she felt disappointed, she did not show it.
>
> If he has a key, he can get into the house.
>
> He will face the facts if he is honest.
>
> If that is the case, then I am wrong.

In all of these expressions of something conditional, we see that there is a part of the sentence that expresses a condition, and a part that gives the result. Each part has its own subject and predicate, but the part that expresses the condition is not a complete thought: "If I work. . . ."; whereas the part which expresses the result ". . . I will succeed" can stand as a complete thought. Such sentences are called *complex sentences*, and you will learn more about them in 7th grade.

Sixth or Seventh Grade

Introduction to Composition

In studying any language, we are studying words, not only single words, as in spelling lists, but words living together as in stories, poems, and the letters we write to our friends. There are many different kinds of words, just as there are many different kinds of people in the world. Just as there are people who are either thinkers or doers, so also are there words which are more connected with thought, others with action. Just as there are sensitive people, artists who take delight in color and music, so are there words which express feeling. When we study some of the words in what we call "the parts of speech," we find that each is like a tiny "sound-mirror" which reflects some one part of human nature.

For instance, what happens when we use a noun? Maybe at night, after going to bed, we see a shadow at the window and hear a strange sound. We lie quite still, a little afraid, wondering what is there. The shadow flies toward us, there is a thump on the bed. It is the *cat*. We are not afraid anymore; we laugh and take the cat in our arms and pet it. Before we recognized the cat and named it, we were quiet, but busy trying to find out what the shadow was. Our thoughts were busy, searching for a *name*! The noun, or name, works in our thinking—our head.

When we use a verb, we are expressing action and the verb is the word which makes us want to use our hands and feet. You all know people who talk "with their hands." Watch them and see how often their hands make gestures in connection with verbs. The more dramatic the tale, the more emphatic the gestures! The verbs in expressions such as these just beg for an accompanying gesture:

"I took aim and fired!"

"You've hit the nail on the head!"

"He raised his sword and struck down the foe!"

I can remember a story I once told to some first graders. The "wicked brother" *kicked* open the door to the poor man's hut. Not even a second after I said *kicked*, one little boy who was listening nearly kicked his desk over. In another story about a little gnome who fell into a deep pit, another listener, a little girl, fell off her chair.

Now let us go a little further. When you hear words like *beautiful, ugly, happy, sad, bright, dark, jolly, cross, gay, mournful*, you can easily separate them into two groups: the *bright* group and the *dark* group. What feelings would you have in relation to each group? Pleasant and unpleasant! These are the words that express feeling, the adjectives, and they reflect the fact that the human being has feelings

So we see how the nouns, the verbs, and the adjectives mirror our thinking, our feelings, and the will that lives in our actions. These three parts of speech, together with all the others, work together in the compositions we write in our English studies. What are compositions? They are actually stories about what we have done, or felt, or thought!

Let us compare a composition with something we know. The whole composition can be compared with a day full of events (let us say a day at school). When we look back at such a day, there is the beginning. Something we might have done at the very beginning, or not have done, has its effect later in the day. For example, the other day John left his lunch box at home. Each day has some moment which is either the best or the worst moment of that day. Then what follows that moment is either better or worse! Finally the end of the day arrives and has its special character. So also, in any written work that we compose, we arrange what we want to say in a definite order. The beginning of the composition points to a special moment, a special thought or event. And the ending of the composition must be as real, as meaningful, as the end of the day.

You all know that paragraphs in a composition should show changes of thought, or of action, just as there are changes in your day as you go from home to school, from class to class, and from work to play.

And within the paragraphs live the sentences. They are the bearers of the thoughts. Each sentence is like a little stage. The actors are the words, and as they play their parts on stage, they act together to give a whole thought.

You all know, that as complete thoughts, each sentence must have a noun (or pronoun) as a subject, a verb as a predicate. Now, if we remember what we have been saying about nouns and thinking, verbs and acting, we can make up a more picturesque rule about sentences: every sentence must have a head, and arms and legs; but like a human being who has no heart, no feelings, a sentence without adjectives is cold and unfriendly. Some examples: *The moon rose. The wind blew.* Or: *The silvery moon rose. The soft wind blew.* Noun, verb, and adjective show how closely the parts of speech are related to the human being.

A Story for a Lesson on Nouns

A man was lost in a jungle. He didn't know which way to turn, for the underbrush was too thick to see through and the leaves overhead hid the sky. As he stood wondering what to do, he heard a noise. At first it sounded very far away. Then it came nearer and nearer, growing louder and louder. He didn't know what it was and that made him uncertain. If only he could have named the thing that seemed to be coming toward him so rapidly, he would have known what to do so as to protect himself.

First he thought it was a roaring wind, so he lay flat on the ground and put his arms around the roots of a tall tree Then he thought, "No! It sounds more like water flooding over the land." He jumped up in a hurry and started to climb the tree. In his fearful hurry he scratched his hands and shins and tore his pants. Up he went, hand over hand, until he reached a high branch. He rested but a moment for the sound became louder, more frightening, like the roar of a gorilla leaping toward him through the thick treetops. In a flash the man started down the tree again. As soon as he reached the ground, his heart nearly failed him. Now the sound seemed to come from the underbrush and it was so like the roar of a lion that he started up the tree again. The poor man was beside himself with terror, all because he couldn't name the thing!

Lion? Gorilla? Wind? Flood? Each name made all the difference to him as to whether he should go up or come down, to save himself. If he had been able to name it right off, he wouldn't have lost his wits; he would have been able to use his presence of mind, to keep calm, to know what to do in relation to the sound.

You ask, "How did the story end?" That I could only tell you if I knew what it was that had made the fearful sound!

When we can name a thing, we know where it stands in relation to us. Have you ever bumped into something in the dark? How comforting it is when you find out, "It was only a chair!" Or when you see some object that you have never seen before, can you rest until you find out what it is, or how to use it?

(Here the teacher can show the class some objects which he is sure are new to the children. Real curiosity is aroused. They experience what it feels like *not to know* what something is.)

Whenever we see something new and strange, something we can't name, we feel uneasy. Once we can name it, we feel secure. We seldom think how much of our knowledge depends on being able to name what we see, hear, taste and smell.

The nouns, or names, give us a ground of knowledge to stand on. Each noun carries in it some knowledge of what we do with what we name:

apple or pincushion
telescope or microscope
rake or shovel
boat or sled
sword or plow
vinegar or sugar
salt or syrup
lemon or honey

What a variety of actions each of these nouns calls to mind!

Assignment
Write a short story, recalling some experience you have had when you found out what some *new* sight, or strange sound, really was.

A Lesson on Verbs

When we use a noun, we are naming something. That means we know what it is, where it belongs, how we can use it or protect ourselves from it. In a sense, to be able to name something, we have to step far enough away from it to be able to see it, to have a good look at it. We separate ourselves from something so as to name it!

Verbs give us quite another experience which you can see for yourselves if you watch people when they are talking. See how they use their hands!

Just recently I was listening to and watching a little girl as she described one of her first rides on her new bicycle:

"We *climbed* a hill, *coasted* down the other side and *curved* suddenly around at the bottom of the hill so fast that we nearly sliced up a tree."

With every verb, she made a gesture with her hands.

Verbs also get into a person's feet, as you will hear in this story about:

"The Poor Hindu and the Pot of Curds" (an Indian Folk Tale)

A poor Hindu, walking along, came upon a dead mouse. Just then a wise man passed by and said, "Any decent young fellow, with his wits about him, has only to pick that mouse up, and he might start a business and keep a wife." The poor Hindu heard this. So he picked up the mouse, took it to a nearby tavern and sold it for a farthing for the tavern cat. With the farthing he bought some molasses and took it, with a pot of drinking water, to the edge of the forest where he met some flower-gatherers. He gave them each a little molasses and some water. In return they gave him a handful of flowers. These he sold for three farthings, bought more molasses and went back the next day to the flower-gatherers who gave him in exchange flowering plants—buds, roots and all! He sold these for eight farthings.

On his way home he was caught in a wind storm. It blew down many branches and cluttered up the King's garden. The gardener didn't know how to clear them away. The poor Hindu said he would do it in return for the wood. Then he paid a lot of children with molasses, and they cleared up the garden for him.

He sold the wood to a potter for his fire and got sixteen farthings. Now with twenty-four farthings he felt very rich. He thought he should do something on a grander scale. Just then he met a man carrying a pot of curds (made from goat-milk). He bought the pot of curds and took it home. Then after eating his fill and finding quite a bit left, he settled down happily to plan what to do next.

He said to himself, "I can sell these curds for enough to buy a goat. With the milk of my goat I can sell enough to buy two more goats. Soon I shall have a large herd. I will have to build a shed for the herd. And I shall build myself a new house—a fine house. After that I shall find myself a wife. She will be so beautiful that many men will be jealous of me. I will dress her in the finest silks and give her the finest jewels. She shall have everything she wants; but if she doesn't obey me and do everything I tell her to do, I will push her down the steps!" With that he pushed the pot of curds so violently that it turned upside down and all his dreams splashed away with the curds.

This story gives a true picture of what happens when we use verbs. Whether or not we act them out, as the poor Hindu did, we nevertheless have a tendency to do so. If we gave in to that tendency, we would get very tired, for our hands and feet would be as busy as our tongues. Verbs make us' feel like acting them out.,

Which of you will volunteer to act out the verbs in a little story I shall tell? (Or here the teacher can select a phlegmatic child.)

"Mary *hurried* into the room. She *ran* to her own desk, *pulled* her chair aside and *picked* up three pencils that were lying on the floor. She *placed* them in her pencil box and *pushed* her chair back into place. She *skipped* over to the other side of the room and *lifted* the heavy dictionary from the floor and *heaved* it back up on its shelf. Then she *hopped* over to the blackboard, *stooped* down and *picked* up two erasers that were on the floor and *put* them back in the tray. Then she *ran* to the closet and *found* the dustcloth, *hurried* back and *dusted* the floor. When it was clean, she *jumped* up and *danced* back to the closet. She *hung* up the dustcloth on its peg. Now the room looked neat!"

Introduction to Four Elements of Poetry

In eurythmy we step to four different rhythms which express courage, gaiety, sadness and thoughtfulness. In poetry these rhythms are called the meters, and the single measure that is repeated in the poem is called the foot. Just as our feet follow the rhythm in eurythmy, so the poem follows a certain meter which helps to give us the' mood of the poem. The Greek names for the four main meters in poetry are the *iambus*, the *trochee* the *anapest* and the *dactyl*.

The iambus, and the anapest are rising rhythms, with a long beat following the short. The trochee and the dactyl give the long beat first and fall off with the short. Hence they are spoken of as falling rhythms.

In the iambus we feel similar to what a soldier feels when courageously he attacks the enemy,

A steed! a steed of matchlesse speede,
A sword of metal keene!
All else to noble heartes is drosse,
All else on earth is meane.
　　　　　—William Motherwell

In the trochee there is a quieter feeling. The battle is over and the soldier can rest and even sleep, forgetful of danger and fighting.

Soldier, rest! Thy warfare o'er,
Sleep the sleep that knows not breaking;
Dream of battlefields no more,
Days of danger, nights of waking.
　　　　　—Sir Walter Scott

The anapest is a lively, dancing meter, and one feels in it a lively, harmonious mood.

> Oh, who is so merry, so merry, heigh ho!
> As the light-hearted fairy, heigh, heigh ho!
> He dances and sings
> To the sound of his wings,
> With a hey, and a heigh and a ho!

In the dactyl we feel more sober than we do in the anapest. If the anapest is like a lighthearted fairy, the dactyl is like the chief or ruler of a people who walks among them with great dignity.

> Hail to the Chief who in triumph advances!
> Honor'd and bless'd be the evergreen pine!
> Long may the tree, in his banner that glances,
> Flourish, the shelter and grace of our line!

There are four elements which, woven together, form a poem and we should keep them all in mind.

We might call the first one the *sense* of the poem, for both feeling and thought must inspire it and give it sense.

Once we have the sense of the poem we can choose the *meter* that helps to express it. The *rhymes* can then be worked out, but they must not destroy the sense. The fourth element lies in the *sounds* of all the words, for we can find many words so lively in their sounds that they help us to get the meaning and mood of the poem.

Hindu Proverbs—Examples for the Four Kinds of Sentences

Declarative

> In a strong position even a coward is a lion.
> He alone lives on who gathers fame.
> Though not your kin, a friend is your best relation.

Good men go on despite calamities.
Giving is in the power of the giver.
A wise man sticks to his own station.
The Earth feels no evil.
A good son is the light of the family.

Imperative

Stick to one thing and all will come.
Aim at everything and all will go.

Learn the good ways of your enemies
Avoid the bad ways of your elders.

Hold on to your luggage and walk slowly.
Always act as the people desire.
Be a brother to the good.

Interrogative

How far can you push a person upon a tree?
Must you teach your grandfather how to cough?
Who can get the better of fate?
Is a lamp pleasing to the blind?

Exclamatory

An elegant shop, but the sweets they sell are tasteless!
I am come from Delhi and my brother tells me the news!
God's most wondrous deeds: one moment sunshine,
            another moment shade!
No delight like misery when it doesn't last long!

Seventh Grade

Why Study English?

The wise Roman, Marcus Aurelius, once said, "Say and do everything in conformity with the soundest reason. For such a purpose frees man from trouble and warfare and all artifice and ostentatious display."

In simpler words: say and do everything according to the soundest reason, for then you will avoid trouble, war, make-believe and showing off.

How can we understand this better?

The wise man was probably like everyone else when he was a baby. He couldn't reason and think. At a certain young age he probably knew four words (not many more) well: "I don't want to."

When a three-year-old is asked to do something, he says "I don't want to." Those being his words, he doesn't think beyond them. If he is still told to wash his hands before eating, he gets angry and cries and yells and has to be disciplined.

As he grows older he learns to speak and think a little more reasonably. When told to do something, he is able to say, "I don't want to, but if I must, I must." He doesn't get as angry anymore.

When he is yet older, he thinks and speaks even more wisely, saying, "I don't want to, but perhaps I am wrong. Maybe I will learn something I don't yet know if I do this that I don't really want to do."

When we study English, the language of our own land, we are learning how to think clearly and wisely so that we can understand ourselves and the world around us, and can then act, as Marcus Aurelius said "in conformity with the soundest reason," so as to avoid anger and war, and to be natural people who can meet others without pretending or showing off.

Adverbs

A Dictation

Jonathan walked slowly up the road until he reached the house. Then he stopped and looked around. It was a very old house. First he saw that part of the roof had blown away. Next he stepped carefully up the rotting steps. After he had peeked through the broken window panes, he stood still and listened. The shutters were loose and swung so creakingly in the wind that the whole house sounded remarkably like an old woman scolding him for stepping on her toes.

Underline all those words in this little story that tell you *how*, *when*, and *where* something happened. These are the adverbs.

Let us compare adverbs with adjectives. Adjectives give color, shape, mood, and feeling to a description. Through them we can show what we feel. Adverbs, by expressing how or when or where something takes place, have to be true to the facts. We cannot say that Tommy comes *early* to school when the fact is that he usually arrives *late*.

In our story about Jonathan, the adverbs: *slowly, around, carefully, still, creakingly,* and *remarkably,* all give a more definite meaning to the verbs, the actions. The adverbs *first* and *next* express the exact order of events. Then there are *so* and *very* which express how old, how creakingly the house appears and acts. Through them we can see that adverbs also modify adjectives and other adverbs.

Adjectives can express one's inner mood, adverbs are more often true to outer facts, especially when they modify verbs. Those that modify adjectives and other adverbs come closer to expressing inner feeling. This you can see in the following examples:

I stepped back *very* quietly. (Maybe someone else would not think so.)

My coat is *too* heavy. (Perhaps you are just tired out.)

I saw him *twice* in one day. (That is an exact count!)

Adverbs that express when and where something takes place have to be true to outer events because they refer to time and place. How something happens, as expressed in adverbs like *so, very, exceedingly, too,* and *slightly*—can depend on one's inner judgment and mood.

To remember

An adverb is a word that makes more definite the meaning of a verb, an adjective, or another adverb. Adverbs tell how, when or where something occurs.

For homework

Write the story of an event in your own experience, making use of adverbs to express exactly when and where and even how it all happened.

Practice in distinguishing adverbs and adjectives

Underline the adjectives in green, the adverbs in orange. Draw an arrow from each adjective or adverb to the word it modifies.

Come early.

The early bird catches the worm.

The girl is well now so she does her work well.

The rowers pulled hard but, with the wind against them,
      they found it a hard task to reach the shore.

Though a fast ship, it did not go fast owing to the fog.

I waited long for the train and it was a long trip.

He laughs best who laughs last.

The last book I read was also the best one.

(The three degrees of comparison of adverbs should be studied as given in any grammar text.)

Identifying the Parts of Speech

Put list of words on the blackboard:

	Verbs change to nouns.
cut	I cut my finger
	The cut was not deep.
walk	They walk slowly.
	It is a long walk.
jump	I jump over the wall.
	The jump landed me in a haystack.
work	We work hard.
	Hard work never killed anybody
	Nouns change to adjectives
garden	Jim was digging in the garden.
	The garden door was open.
copper	Copper is a useful metal.
	Copper nails don't rust.
light	The light of the sun is the greatest light.
	Her light hair reminds me of the sun.
blue	The blue of the sky is like her eyes.
	Her blue dress is the color of the sea.
	Adjectives change to verbs.
warm	We are not having warm weather.
	Warm the milk.
wet	The wet leaves dripped all afternoon.
	She fell in the pool and wet her best dress.
picture	The picture book belongs to my brother.
	Can you picture her in her mother's long dress?

Have children discover for themselves what each group of words does. Discuss with them how the sentence makes the words change. Each word alone is not sure of what it can do, but as soon as it gets together with other words, it knows what it can do. This is very much like a human being. One person alone cannot do very much. He has to join in with others to find out how many different abilities he has.

Rule

The way a word is used in a sentence tells us what part of speech it is.

Introducing the Study of Pronouns

Some people like to talk a lot, to talk without thinking. Just such a person, Mrs. O'Fidget, never had a thought when she was alone, but as soon as she caught sight of anyone she knew, she would start to talk as fast as she could.

One day, sitting on her front porch in her rocking chair, she saw Mrs. O'Hara coming by. Mrs. O'Fidget slipped from her rocker, as quick as an eel, and down the steps to the side-walk just in time to put a stop to Mrs. O'Hara's journey with a few words.

Now Mrs. O'Hara had to listen, first standing on one foot, then on the other. Her back began to ache, her head swam, her eyelids felt heavy, for she could not understand what Mrs. O'Fidget was saying. And this is part of what she said. Can you understand it?

"Did you know that Mr. Moriarty broke his leg this morning coming down his brother's steps? He was sitting on the porch, and when he fell down the steps he ran after him, and he said he never knew anyone to fall down those steps before. So he took him up on the porch. I could hear his loud groans. His wife wasn't even home. She was over at Mrs. Murphy's, so she never knew about it. Just as she was asking her all about her daughter's wedding, the doorbell rang and. . . ."

What makes Mrs. O'Fidget's story so hard to follow? Too many pronouns. How would you make it clearer? By using names of people more often. You will often hear people who fail to make themselves clear because they do not show to whom their pronouns refer. Too many pronouns destroy meaning. Each pronoun should refer clearly to a noun which may be a person's name.

A good rule to put into practice is that a pronoun must refer to the last preceding noun in a thought.

I would like you to rewrite Mrs. O'Fidget's story so that it makes sense.

Introducing the Study of Adjectives

Watching the sunset, two men once stood together on the shore of the ocean. Although they were good friends, the two were very different. One was tall and thin with sad, dark eyes and slender hands. His friend was short and plump with twinkling blue eyes and ruddy cheeks. After the sun had set, they parted, each going home. It had been such a beautiful sunset that each felt the urge to write something about it.

One wrote as follows:

"The weary sun went down beyond the restless waves. A wailing wind blew over the empty sands and around the lonely cliffs. The hollow sky darkened as the sad night came. One by one, the forlorn stars appeared and shed their feeble light."

The other man wrote:

"The jolly sun went down beyond the dancing waves. A singing wind blew over the golden sands and around the sturdy cliffs. The shining sky darkened as the peaceful night came. One by one the friendly, stars appeared and shed their cheerful light."

Do these sound like descriptions of the same sunset? Can you guess which description was written by which man? As I dictate, write down each description and underline the words that make the descriptions so different.

These words are the adjectives. The adjectives we choose when we describe things often show how we ourselves feel. The sad person sees the sunset in a sad way, the happy one in a happy way.

What do these adjectives do? They describe the sun, the waves, the wind, the cliffs—in other words, the nouns. Now we can remember the rule: An adjective is a word that describes, or modifies, a noun or a pronoun. (He is plump. She is tall. It is good.)

For your homework, write a description in two moods—changing only the adjectives to show the different moods.

Comparison of Adjectives

If we say, "Mary is taller than Ann, but Ann is the older one," what are we doing? We are comparing the two girls.

To compare further, "Mary is tall. Mary is taller than Ann. Mary is the tallest one in the class." We have not only compared two people, but many, and have said that one is the tallest.

- Tall, taller, tallest—each is an adjective which describes a different degree of tallness.
- *Tall* gives a certain, or *positive*, degree.
- *Taller* gives a *comparative* degree, and is used when comparing only two.
- *Tallest* gives a *superlative* degree, and is used when comparing more than two.

Now let us take some adjectives and compare them. We will find that they fall into groups depending on the forms of comparison they take.

Positive	Comparative	Superlative
short	shorter	shortest
slow	slower	slowest
	etc.	
beautiful	more beautiful	most beautiful
courageous	more courageous	most courageous
	etc.	
healthy	healthier	healthiest
happy	happier	happiest
	etc.	
good	better	best
little	less	least
much	more	most
	etc.	
sad	sadder	saddest
red	redder	reddest
	etc.	

Now that you have found that adjectives fall into groups, when they are compared, can you describe these groups?

1. Adjectives of one syllable form the comparative by adding *–er*, and the superlative by adding *–est*.

2. Adjectives of three or more syllables use *more* and *most* with the positive.

3. Most adjectives ending in "y" change the "y" to "i" before adding *–er* or *–est*.

4. Some adjectives form the comparative and superlative by using different words.

5. One syllable adjectives that end in a single consonant preceded by one vowel double the final consonant before adding *–er* and *–est*.

You will also find that some adjectives can be compared either by adding *–er* and *–est*, or by using *more* and *most*.

Compare the following adjectives, placing them in their proper groups.

angry	courteous	gentle	lucky
big	cruel	good	manly
boastful.	dangerous	handsome	many
careless	dim	juicy	noble
comfortable	dull	hot	pleasant

Picture-making Words

If we look at a written word, we see the shapes of the letters and that they are either beautifully written or not, but if they spell a word whose meaning we do not know, they tell us nothing. If we know the meaning and can see that, despite the letters, then the word can provide us with a kind of picture.

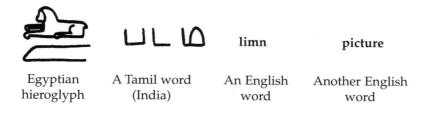

| Egyptian hieroglyph | A Tamil word (India) | An English word | Another English word |

When you look at each of these four examples of writing, you will see that the picture is in the writing in the case of the hieroglyph. The characters in the Tamil word tell you nothing. The letters are pah-dah-yim, and the word is pronounced pahdam, and it means 'picture.' The word *limn* is a word you do not know the meaning of, so the letters tell you nothing, until you know that it means to draw or paint a picture. In the last three words, the picture is not in the writing, but in our minds. So it is with our English words, as compared with ancient picture writing. Yet, in English, we experience the picturesque quality of words quite often through the sounds of the words. Some of the words we use are more picturesque than others.

Examples	More picturesque
run	speed, dash, rush, dart, streak
cold	bleak, raw, freezing, nippy, bitter
sad	somber, dismal, gloomy, mournful
cloud	fog, mist, haze, thunderhead, woolpack

In such picture-giving words we notice how each one makes us see a slightly different picture. The more words we learn to use, the more we'll be able to interest others in what we say or write.

It is because we so often do not search for the right word that we overwork a few words. We use them on every occasion. And when we are limited to a few overworked words in order to express the infinite variety of experiences and impressions, we sound dull, and we feel dull.

The overworked words in general are: *good, big, fine, beautiful, nice, awful, great, wonderful, crazy, awfully good, perfectly lovely, absolutely fierce, simply awful, terribly good, very, many, fabulous,* etc.

In the following examples from some of your compositions, I will underline the overworked words, the words that fail to paint a picture.

"Across the street from my house there is a <u>very nice</u> apartment house."

"There are <u>many beautiful</u> snow-covered trees."

"If one walks down the street very early in the morning, one cannot see <u>very</u> many people and the street is <u>very</u> still."

"The people on the block are <u>very nice</u>."

'Our houses are all <u>made</u> of brick. There are two junipers at the end of our walk which is <u>made</u> of pink cement. All the streets were <u>made</u> after we came."

Assignment

Find a more picturesque adjective to replace great, good, nice, and *funny* in the following phrases:

a great man	a good movie	a nice time
a great storm	a good lunch	a nice dress
a great tree	a good neighbor	a nice garden
	a good speech	a nice old lady

a funny story
a funny girl
a funny hat
a funny automobile

Or, describe in a few sentences, using picture-making words—words that will make us feel, taste, see, hear, or smell—one of the following:

- Your room at home.
- Your supper last night.
- Someone you saw on the way to school.
- Something that happened at recess.

Description through Comparison

We often observe things that remind us of other things. A gnarled apple tree reminds us of an old workingman. Apple blossoms make us think of dainty little girls dressed in pink and white. An old house reminds us of an old woman who sits comfortably to watch life go by. When the wind rattles the doors and windows, it sounds as if someone were scolding and complaining.

We often have these impressions, and when we write or talk, we should use them for they make writing or conversation more interesting. They make pictures.

I used to watch a little train coming down a mountain like an old lady trying to keep from running too fast. I used to see a big mountain looking up over the other mountains like a giant with one eye; the trees along its ridge looked like his eyelashes, and the big rocks lower down looked like the giant's teeth.

I am going to give you three ways of describing something, of giving a word-picture. I wonder if you can discover the difference in each.

1. The massive mountain towered high above all the other mountain ridges.
2. The mountain was like a mighty giant who looked out over the surrounding ridges.
3. The mountain was a mighty giant who lifted his head to look out over the surrounding mountains.

or

1. The tiny train ran down the mountain as if it could never stop itself.
2. The train looked like a tiny old lady running downhill so fast that she could not stop herself.
3. It was always amusing to watch that train. The little old lady raced down the hill, holding on to her skirts, shrilling her whistle, panting and chugging and evidently hoping she could come to a stop when she reached the station.

Can you discover the difference that lies in each of these three kinds of description? In the first, the mountain and the train are pictured by using adjectives (*massive, tiny*).

In the second, the picture is given through a comparison. The mountain is like a giant; the train is like a little old lady. We can call this *using a simile.*

In the third description, we do not use the word *like* at all. We turn the train into a lady, the mountain into a giant. But we take it for granted that it is a comparison, not the real thing. This method of comparison is called *metaphor.*

Assignment

Recall something of interest you have seen or heard and describe it in each of the three ways that I have illustrated. Maybe one of the following topics has been an experience in your memory.

The crowing of a rooster.
A weedy garden.
A deserted house.
Rain on the roof.
A sharp wind.
The new leaves of springtime.
An old dilapidated car.

Choose some such impression, describe it directly just using adjectives, describe it with a simile, and describe it in metaphor.

Wish, Wonder and Surprise

(The following pages represent one teacher's efforts to explore and work out the suggestion given in the Waldorf school curriculum for a seventh grade. This teacher, however, carried out these lessons for the first time in an eighth grade. The children were still very much involved in the process of awakening to their inner, personal feelings as well as to new powers of observation of the world around them.)

Wishes

What do you look for, what do you seek?
A silver bird with a golden beak.

What do you long for, what do you crave?
Golden gems in a silver cave.

What do you lack, and what do you need?
A silver sword and a golden steed.

What do you want, of what do you dream?
A golden ship on a silver stream.

What do you have, and what do you own?
A silver robe and a golden crown.

What would you be? Oh, what would you be?
Only the King of the land and the sea.

—Norman Ault

We all have wishes. What do we wish for? What do we seek?

Each one of us has his own wish. Sometimes it is the wish to be like everyone else. Sometimes it is a very different wish from that of our parents or teachers. Sometimes it is a wish for someone else, like a birthday wish. Our wishes come from deep within ourselves. We may wish for a new dress, for a chance to play in a game, for skill in carrying out a certain assignment. We may wish for someone we love who is far away or ill. All of us have the wish for God's help in living as we should. Elizabeth Barrett Browning wrote, "Every wish is like a prayer with God."

Many are the poets who have expressed their wishes in beautiful verse, and I would like you to listen to some of their wishes.

This is my prayer to thee, my lord—
Give me the strength lightly to bear my joys and sorrows.
Give me the strength to make my love fruitful in service.
Give me the strength never to disown the poor or bend
    my knee before insolent might.
Give me the strength to raise my mind high above daily trifles.
And give me the strength to surrender my strength to thy will
    with love.

—Rabindranath Tagore

Invocation to Rain in Summer

O gentle, gentle summer rain,
  Let not the silver lily pine,
The drooping lily pine in vain
  To feel that dewy touch of thine—
To drink thy freshness once again,
O gentle, gentle summer rain.

—W. C. Bennett

The Swing

How do you like to go up in a swing,
Up in the air so blue?
Oh I do think it is the pleasantest thing
Ever a child can do!

Up in the air and over the wall,
Till I can see so wide,
Rivers and trees and cattle and all
Over the countryside—

Till Ilook down on the garden green,
Down on the roof so brown—
Up in the air I go flying again,
Up in the air and down!

—Robert Louis Stevenson

Oh that my grief were thoroughly weighed, and my calamity laid in the balances together!
Oh that I might have my request; and that God would grant me the thing I long for!

—from the *Book of Job,* Chapter 6

Give ear to my prayer, O God; and hide not thyself from my supplication.
Attend unto me, and hear me: I mourn in my complaint, and make a noise;
My heart is sore pained within me: and the terrors of death are upon me.
And I have said, O that I had wings like a dove! for then I would fly away and be at rest.
Lo, then would I wander far off—and remain in the wilderness.
I would hasten my escape from the windy storm and tempest.

—*Psalm 55*

O to sail the sea in a ship!
To leave this steady unendurable land,
To leave the tiresome sameness of the streets, the sidewalks,
and the houses,
To leave you, O you solid, motionless land, and entering a ship,
To sail and sail and sail!
To be a sailor of the world bound for all ports.

—Walt Whitman

(The whole of Walt Whitman's poem "Sea-Drift" can be read to give
the children a touching experience of the longing of a bird for his
mate.)

from *The People, Yes*

I earn my living.
I make enough to get by
and it takes all my time.

If I had more time
I could do more for myself
and maybe for others.
I could read and study
and talk things over
and find out about things.
It takes time. I wish I had the time.

—Carl Sandburg

The children were asked to write down their dearest wishes, with
the promise that, if they asked the teacher not to read their wishes to
the class, those wishes would be held in strict confidence. However,
from among the wishes that were written, it was possible to take
certain sentences and to show the children how to transform them into
expressions of "longing or hope or desire"—to express a wish in terms
that were quite different than in expressing facts. Some examples of
the original statements and their transformation as expressions of
wish are given below:

"I would like to visit the different lands I've studied about."
O for a chance to visit the different lands I've studied about!

"I wish I could grow to know myself as well as worldly things."

May I grow to know myself as well as worldly things.

"I hope there will never be another war, nor cruelty to man or beast."

Let there never be another war, nor cruelty to man or beast.

"I hope I will never take for granted God's gifts to the earth —the sky, the grass, and the animals from the mighty whale to the tiny fly."

God's gifts to the earth—the sky, the grass, and all the animals, from the mighty whale to the tiny fly—may I never take them for granted!

Following these exercises, the children then wrote their wishes in verse, since they had been also studying meter, rhyme, and verse forms in poetry.

Wonder

We think it wonderful if we can do or have what we wish for; but what is the deepest wish of every human being? To find what is true and beautiful and good! And when we find something good, beautiful, and true—then we are filled with wonder.

There is a difference whether we say, "I wonder why," or say, "How wonderful!" The first is really a question; the second is an exclamation. Some other words for wonder are *amazement, reverence, appreciation*.

The scientist, William Beebe, has written, "Now and then we see something which needs no explanation, but demands only appreciation and wonder—"

The artist, the scientist, and the poet experience wonder in varying ways.

Here are three paintings: *The Oncoming Storm* by George Inness, *Toilers of the Sea* by Albert Ryder, and *Oncoming Spring* by Charles Burchfield. Each of these paintings is an expression of the wonder that inspired each artist to paint his picture.

To the naturalist, Donald Culross Peattie, "One square mile of land" was an object of wonder. In an essay on 'What Life Means—an Answer in Nature,' he expresses his sense of wonder:

> How good the air smelled here! How high and taut was the arc of the sky!
>
> One square mile of land—not scenically sensational land, not even some sort of wild-life sanctuary; but just a prairie grove—and it was inhabited, I estimate, by a round million of living, breathing, reproducing, dying beings.
>
> There were earthworms under my feet, penetrating the soil, aerating it, bringing it laboriously to the surface from richer depths. Down there the pine mice had their dwellings and runways and hideouts. A squirrel scolded me from overhead.
>
> The birds in the leaves, the snake under the stone, the spider running zigzag down her shining orb web, the cottontail dashing from the weasel in great heart-bursting bounds of terror, the turtle sunning himself on a log, the thrush at evening turned toward sunset, letting fall his pure syllables of praise—all these affirm that life is worth living.

The poet, William Cullen Bryant, in his "Song of the Stars," imagines a wonder-filled song that they sang together:

When the radiant morn of creation broke—
And the world in the smile of God awoke,

And orbs of beauty and spheres of flame
From the void abyss by myriads came,—

Their silver voices in chorus rung,
And this was the song the bright ones sung.

> Look, look, through our glittering ranks afar,
> In the infinite azure, star after star,
> How they brighten and bloom as they swiftly pass!
> How the verdure runs o'er each rolling mass!
> And the path of the gentle winds is seen,
> Where the small waves dance, and the young woods lean,

And see, where the brighter daybeams pour,
How the rainbows hang in the sunny shower—

(Another expression of wonder, the 8th Psalm, can also be read.)

The children were asked to write about something that had filled them with wonder. This called upon their powers of observation as well as the quality of appreciativeness. One pupil wrote a composition entitled "The Eternal Miracle." She described the changes wrought by the four seasons. The last paragraph read:

"As I stood there. I wondered to myself. I wondered at the changes I had seen during the past year; I wondered at the buds and flowers and how they had turned from lifeless, brown, ugly stalks to beautiful, bright, delicate flowers and leaves; and as I stood there, I was filled with awe."

When she converted those thoughts into verse, the last verse was developed as follows:

It was autumn, crisp and lively,
    and the leaves were painted gay.
Brown and yellow, red, and orange,
    in a beautiful array.
All the animals were cozy,
    in their winter homes were curled,
And I stood there and I wondered
    At the beauty of the world.

From what the children wrote in their compositions, exercises were developed in ways of expressing wonder, such as:

How lofty was the soaring of that hawk!
With what tireless effort the ants were working!
There it loomed, a gigantic shadow upon the clouds!
See how the ocean licks along the shore!

Surprise

What do we feel when something unexpected happens? Surprise! We have all had surprises. We remember the happy surprises especially, for years afterwards. But there have also been unhappy surprises, and through them we have often learned more than through the happy ones. You are not yet old enough to have experienced the way in which the unexpected events in life are often the turning points in a person's fate. But I can look back and trace the seemingly chance events that led to this moment when I stand here in this room with you. Many people suffer a sense of defeat when their carefully laid plans go wrong. They do not allow the "unexpected" to happen; but with the surprises of life often come the most decisive happenings.

I have found three little stories, or parts of stories, that will tell you how variously the unexpected events have their effect on the feelings' and actions of people. You may find other such examples.

from *A New England Auction*

"The house was very poor. An old man had lived there for years alone, and everything was grimy with dirt.

After the auction was over, they took out his mattress and a lot of old quilts to burn them back of the house. They were so dirty no one wanted them, of course.

Well the joke of it was, no sooner did the fire get started than they found the bedding was full of money. Bills went up in the air like burning leaves—dollar bills and five-dollar bills, and ten-dollar bills—all of them burning! Of course the men tried to put out the fire. That mattress was just about stuffed with bills. But pshaw! they couldn't put it out. They had to stand there and watch all of that money go up in the air.

And Mrs. Sherman laughs again at the jokes Fate plays on people.

—Elizabeth Coatsworth

from *Yankee Almanac*

There were two brothers on our road who quarreled over some apples as big boys. No one knows exactly what the apples had to do with it. At any rate the boys stopped speaking to each other. As time went on, they married and had families. One inherited the family farm and the other went to live at the place next door. One had stock but no barn. The other had a barn but no stock. In some way arrangements were made so that the stock should be kept in the barn. A dozen times a week the two men must have passed close to each other, and renewed their satisfaction in not speaking! Undoubtedly it became a grim game, likely to go on until death entered in.

But here fate intervened. When they were elderly men, one of them was in an apple tree and the other was passing along the road.

The man in the road suddenly yelled: "Look out. You're sawing off the limb you're sitting on!"

The warning was given, the silence was broken, and from that day on the brothers spoke to each other. An apple tree had healed the wound an apple tree had made."

from *The Importance of Being Kobotchnik*

"The dog disappeared. No sign of him for three, four days, a week. I thought he was run over. . . .

About a month after the dog disappeared, I was in Fitchburg one afternoon, and who yelled at me from his car by the curb but the Finn that gave me the dog! . . .

The Finn told me my dog come back to him. Nurmi was alive! He went back on the farm where he was born. I never thought he would do that. It was thirty-one miles away.

Was I glad? I was so glad I could of cried."

—Louis Adamic

When we wish to express surprise, we must leave out all but the sharp experience of the surprise itself. Brief exclamations, questions, commands, and even incomplete sentences, help to express what we feel.

Examples:

Who should it be but my old friend Sam! There he stood as big as life! How on earth had he reached London? What a pleasure! Little did I expect to see him!

Look at the sky, it's clearing up!

She appeared, as if by magic, out of nowhere!

Watch that! It's a perfect home-run! He made it! He made it! What a guy!

I goofed!

Now I know!

How did you know?

I found it! I found it! My school bag!

So that's it!

Look! Look! Another and another!

Behold, the true meaning!

Well done!

I never thought it could happen!

A Teacher's Surprises

(The following exclamations, questions, comments, all were familiar crises in the class, and were met with profound understanding as to the exact nature of a certain kind of surprise!)

I looked at the paper. How neat! How clear! Every letter readable! Whose could it be? Not a misspelled word. How marvelous! How unexpected! Who? No! Not Karen!

Well of all things! Susan has found it out. Proper nouns should be capitalized.

Not a word! Not a single sound! A silent participant in all learning! That's Peter!

Look at John! He is beaming with joy! How nice! He has found the right average!

It Was a Surprise

A composition by a pupil of the class:

". . . Suddenly out of the corner of my eye, I saw a pigeon! It was sitting, not two feet away from me, on the railing of the stairs. The most surprising thing about it was that it did not fly away. It just sat there. It was looking at me, too, very carefully . . .

The pigeon was obviously hurt, so I went inside to find out whether I could bring it in. When I returned, the pigeon looked up as if it recognized me. I took a step toward it when, what do you think, it flew off the railing onto the sidewalk! It gave me a very hurt look over its shoulder, and then sauntered off amid the passersby.

Well, don't think you'll ever catch me meddling in the affairs of a pigeon again!"

Another Experience of Surprise

Little stories in anecdote form are good examples of the element of surprise in our lives; Their style is to have a surprise ending which can bring humor into an otherwise serious story.

Example:

A breakfast guest at the White House during the Coolidge administration was astonished to see the President pour his beverage from cup to saucer. Not to be outdone, the guest followed suit.

The President put cream and sugar in the saucer, and tasted the mixture with his spoon.

The guest was about to do likewise when Mr. Coolidge set the saucer on the floor for the dog.

More Experiences of Wonder

The artist, the naturalist, the poet are all inspired by the experience of wonder and express it in their paintings, in prose and in poetry.

Leonardo da Vinci worked to discover the wondrous working of the human eye and the power of sight. In his notebooks he wrote details of the results of this study and ended with these words:

"Who would believe that so small a space (the eye) could contain the images of all the universe? O mighty process! What talent can avail to penetrate a nature such as these? What tongue will it be that can unfold so great a wonder? Verily, none! This it is that guides the human discourse to the considering of divine things.

Here the figures, here the colors, here all the images of every part of the universe are contracted to a point.

O what point is so marvelous!

O wonderful, O stupendous Necessity, thou, by thy law constrainest all effects to issue from their causes in the briefest possible way!

These are the miracles . . .

Wonder results from observation and discovery of the realities that are at work in the world around us, and in ourselves.

The World Creator moves
In Sun light and in soul light—
In wide world—space without
And soul-depths here within
                    —Rudolf Steiner

When Galileo Galilei, in 1610, fashioned a primitive telescope and trained it upon the moon' s mountains and valleys, he could estimate the heights of tie peaks from the length of their shadows. He wrote:

I am quite beside myself with wonder and I am infinitely grateful to God that it pleased Him to permit me to discover such great marvels as were unknown to all preceding centuries.

from "Of Man and the Moon," *Reader's Digest*, October 1969

On Sunday, July 20th, 1969, Neil Armstrong reached out his booted left foot and planted the first human footprint on the moon. His first utterance was a statement of wonder, "One small step for man, one giant leap for mankind."

On their return flight to earth, Buzz Aldrin quoted a verse from the Psalms (Ps. 8:3-4) to express what his feelings had been during the moon-flight:

"When I consider thy heavens, the work of thy fingers, the moon and the stars which thou hast ordained, what is man that thou art mindful of him?"

—Robert O'Brien,

from an ancient gravestone inscription

"The wonder of the world, the beauty and the power, the shape of things, their colors, lights and shades, these I saw. Look ye also while life lasts."

from a naturalist and author

"Each of you has the whole wealth of the universe at your door. All that I ever had, or still have, may be yours by stretching forth your hand."

—*John Burroughs*

from a renowned scientific traveler

How vivid is the impression produced by the calm of nature at noon in these burning climates! The beasts of the forest retire to the thickets; the birds hide themselves beneath the foliage of the trees or in the crevices of the rocks. Yet amidst this apparent silence, when we lend an attentive ear to the most feeble sounds transmitted through the air, we hear a dull vibration, a continual murmur, a hum of insects filling all the lower strata of the air. Nothing is better fitted to make man feel the extent and power of organic life. Myriads of insects creep upon the soil and flutter round the plants parched by tie heat of the sun. A confused noise issues from every bush, from the decayed trunks of trees, from the clefts of rocks and from the ground undermined by lizards, millipedes, and worm-like amphibians. There are so many voices proclaiming to us that all nature breathes-, and that, under a thousand different forms, life is diffused throughout the cracked and dusty soil as well as in the waters and in the air that circulates around us.

—Alexander Von Humboldt

Written in March
    The cock is crowing,
    The stream is flowing,
    The small birds twitter,
    The lake doth glitter,
The green field sleeps in the sun;
    The oldest and youngest
    Are at work with the strongest,
    The cattle are grazing,
    Their heads never raising;
There are forty feeding like one!

—William Wordsworth

A Vagabond Song

There is something in the autumn that is native to my blood—
Touch of manner, hint of mood;
And my head is like a rhyme,
With the yellow and the purple and the crimson keeping time.

The scarlet of the maples can shake me like a cry
Of bugles going by.
And my lonely spirit thrills
To see the frosty asters like a smoke upon the hills.

There is something in October sets the gypsy blood astir;
We must rise and follow her,
When from every hill of flame
She calls and calls each vagabond by name.

—Bliss Carman

Expressions of Wish

Prayers

We ask, O Lord, that wherever children of Thine touch life, they may leave it richer for having touched it. May they help to make better homes and better schools. May they be kept from cheap and shoddy words. May they have that singleness of heart which will enable them to become more and more aware of God, and then may they, with skill and devotion, make peace between other men and God.

—E.J. Bosworth

from *Gitanjali* (Gitanjali means "Song offerings")

Where the mind is without fear and the head is held high;
Where knowledge is free;
Where the world has not been broken up into fragments by narrow domestic walls;
Where words come out from the depths of truth;
Where the tireless striving stretches its arms towards perfection;
Where the clear stream of reason has not lost its way into the dreary desert sand of dead habit;
Where the mind is led forward by thee into ever-widening thought and action into that heaven of freedom, my Father, let my country awake.

—R. Tagore

"The Prayer of the Donkey" from *Prayers from the Ark*

O God, who made me to trudge along the road always,
to carry heavy loads always,
and to be beaten always!
Give me great courage and gentleness.
One day let somebody understand me—
that I may no longer want to weep
because I can never say what I mean

and they make fun of me.
Let me find a juicy thistle—
and make them give me time to pick it.
And Lord, one day, let me find again
my little brother of the Christmas crib.
                                    —deGasztold

Wishes in Poems

from *Home Thoughts from Abroad*

Oh, to be in England
Now that April's there,
And whoever wakes in England
Sees, some morning, unaware,
That the lowest boughs and the brushwood leaf
Round the elm tree bole are in tiny leaf—
While the chaffinch sings on the orchard bough
In England—now!
                                    —Robert Browning

from *My Heart's in the Highlands*

My heart's in the Highlands, my heart is not here;
My heart's in the Highlands a-chasing the deer;
Chasing the wild deer and following the roe,
My heart's in the Highlands wherever I go.
Wherever I wander, wherever I rove
The hills of the Highlands forever I love.
                                    —Robert Burns

from *A Song of Joy*

O to make the most jubilant song!
Full of music—full of manhood, womanhood, infancy!
Full of common employments—full of grain and trees.

O to go back to the place where I was born.
To hear the birds sing once more.
To ramble about the house and barn and over the fields
    once more.
And through the orchard and along the old lanes once more.

—Walt Whitman

O For a Booke—Old English

O for a Booke and a shadie nooke
    eyther in-a-doore or out;
With the grene leaves whispering overhede,
    or the Streete cryes all about.
Where I maie Reade all at my ease,
    both of the Newe and Olde;
For a jollie goode Booke whereon to looke,
    is better to me than Golde.

A Lesson in Expressing Wishes

Of these three wishes, which should come first?

- The wish for peace on earth?
- The wish for food for those who are hungry?
- The wish for brotherliness amongst humankind?

In a class discussion questions can be raised such as:

- What is brotherliness based on?
- What makes for happiness?
- Why are there hungry people, homeless, and poor?

Then it can be pointed out that if one expresses a wish in terms of oneself, that is—just making the statement, "I wish that there would be peace on earth,"—it is somewhat egotistical. One can form the wish with more humility, expressing a *mood* connected with the wish, a mood of longing, of prayerfulness.

There are ways of expression that leave "I" out of the statement and bring about such a mood at the start.

If only—
Let there be—
May it come to pass—
Oh that—
Would that—
O for—
(and so on)

A composition can then be assigned, using these three wishes and imagining all that would be involved in helping them to come true. A second task would then be to transform the compositions into verse.

The Mood in Verbs

A follow-up of lessons in expressions of wish

Discuss again the egotistical and humble moods in such expressions as:

I hope that your wish *comes* true.
May your wish *come* true.

I wish I could say that I *am* up to date in my homework.
May I soon *be* up to date in my homework!

I wish that he *was* here.
If only he *were* here!

I wish you *were* on our side.
Could you but *be* on our side!

With the change of mood of expression comes a change in what is called the "mood" of the verb. In all, a verb has three moods:

Indicative	He brings me the book.
Imperative	Bring me the book.
Subjunctive	Oh, if he but bring me the book.

Indicative	Spring comes lightly over the hills.
Imperative	Come, Spring, lightly over the hills
Subjunctive	May Spring come lightly over the hills.

Many such examples can be developed in oral practice until the children notice how the verb changes, especially in expressing Wish, from the Indicative Mood to the Subjunctive. They can then write into their notebooks a comparative conjugation of the verb *to be*.

Present Tense

Indicative mood	*Subjunctive mood*
I am.	If I be—
	May I be—
	Might I be—
You are.	If you be—etc.
He is.	If he be—etc.
We are.	If we be—etc.
They are.	May they be—

Past Tense

Indicative mood	*Subjunctive mood*
I was.	If I were—
You were.	If you were—
He was.	If he were—
We are.	If we were—
They are.	If they were—

Book Review Outline • Seventh Grade

I.   Location and period of the story.

Describe the character of the hero or heroine.

Relate some incident that tested his character, showing how he met the test.

II. Outline, or summarize, the plot of the story.

How did the author create suspense? Quote an example.

III. Why did you choose to read this book? Did it hold your interest? What parts interested you most?

What, in your opinion, inspired the author to write it?

IV. Describe the leading characters in the story in connection with its climax.

Tell why, in your opinion, they acted as they did, and what might have happened if they had not taken that action.

Book Review Outline • Eighth Grade

I.   Introduce locale and main characters through the opening incidents. Indicate the plot so as to interest others in reading the book.

or

II. Summarize the plot in terms of the leading character, up to the point of climax, or turning point, of the story, but do not divulge the way the story ends.

Comment on what the author wants to bring out through the characters.

III. Characterize the leading character.

Describe that individual's actions in a critical moment in the story, so as to illustrate his or her qualities, traist or attributes.

Bring out a concluding thought of your own as to why you were sympathetic toward this character.

In general

- Avoid vague endings, sudden ones, or ones that trail off into nothing.
- When necessary explain the connection between the title and the story.
- Try not to retell the whole story.

Eighth Grade

Speech and Song

A talk at the beginning of a block in Main Lesson English

When we study our language, we concern ourselves with spelling, grammar, composition, poetry—and if I were to say that there is one element of language which must necessarily be there, before anything else, what would you say that it is?

Let the children try to think of it.

Words!

At the beginning, then, we will learn something about the history and mystery of words.

In St. John's Gospel we read—

1:1 In the beginning was the Word, and the Word was with God, and the Word was God.

1:14 And the Word was made flesh and dwelt among us, (and we beheld his glory, the glory as of the only begotten of the Father), full of grace and truth.

We may find it hard to realize what these words mean: "the Word was God" and "the Word was made flesh." At least we may think that since God is the Creator of heaven and earth, the Word must take part in forming the earth and the heavens—and all the beings that dwell therein: that God's wisdom in creating the world is his Word. This is something that needs wisdom to understand, and you will not understand it all at once. You may understand that little part of it, which we will discover when we pay attention to the history of the Word—or words.

Before there was writing, there was speech, and in the earliest days it was more song than speech. Speech, as we know it today, is quite different form what it was long, long ago. Today we are more interested in the meaning of a word, whereas men of old understood words through their sounds, somewhat in the same way as we now listen to and understand music. Song and speech were once more nearly the same thing. Now they are divided. As men became more aware of the material world, their words became more prosaic, less musical, more concerned with meanings, less concerned with sounds. And so, today, on the one hand we have our everyday speech, while on the other we have poetry and song, which have in them still a reminder of olden times.

What did men sing of, in those olden times? When he uttered his song, a man would not feel, "I am producing music" as he would today. Rather, he felt, "I am living in music produced by the gods." Thus men, in their song-speech, conversed about the gods and the events taking place among the gods. They felt that whatever sounds they uttered were "sacrifices" to the gods; and in offering their speech to the gods, they felt that they were bringing the gods nearer to the earth.

Then men were aware that if they spoke of cherries and grapes, they must use earthly words; while if they spoke of the gods, they must sing. They felt that the words about the gods should be pronounced slowly; that if they were pronounced too fast they were killed. They began to say, "All music on earth can only be a copy of the heavenly music which began with the creation of humanity." The more religious part of humanity felt that human beings had begun to lose touch with the heavenly music because man was becoming more and more desirous of earthly pleasures: eating, drinking, wearing rich clothes, building luxurious houses and so on. They felt that if men wished to regain their sense of heavenly music—the "Word"—they must make their lives pure and their words living and full of music.

Even when writing was developed, it had to be done in a certain way, for it was writing of holy script. If a religious scribe, in Egypt, wrote a religious word in the wrong way, the Pharaoh would execute him. In the north of England there is today a Bible written by the hands of four or five generations of monks. This was the holy work which took them 450 years, and each monk sacrificed his lifetime to it.

Even in the 10th and 11th centuries after Christ, religious men knew that music and song came from the Divine Creator, God. Almost all music was written, sung, and played for religious reasons, to be offered in the old sense of sacrifice in religious services. These men claimed that before singers produced tones they should purify themselves, free themselves from the earthly appetites and the desire for earthly possessions; that they should make a change from ordinary earthly language (about cherries and grapes), and lift themselves from everyday language to music, in order to draw close to the Spirit of God. For this reason a prayer was pronounced before singing the sacred music. It was a prayer to St. John, for he was looked to as one who could hear the heavenly music.

And this was the prayer:

"Ut queant laxis resonare fibris mire gestorum, famuli tuorum solve pollute labii reatum, S.J."

"In order that thy servant may sing with liberated vocal chords, pardon the offences of the lips which have become earthly (capable of speech), Saint John."

The names of musical notation were carefully hidden in this verse: ut re mi fa sol la si (S.J.). These names are familiar to you when you think of *ut* as *doh*.

When we read the poetic literature that reflects the past as we have come to know it through our study of history, we find echoes of the changes that took place in man's attitude toward heaven and earth.

The ancient Indians longed for the heavenly worlds. They did not feel at home on earth and they sought to unite themselves with God. In their songs they called Him "Beloved," and they sought Him in their own souls. All the things of the outer world were unreal to them when compared to the "Beloved" Who dwelt within.

"Thou who knowest my inmost self, Beloved,
Who knowest myself,
They sell parched grain in the market—
If thou comest to my house, then would I tell thee
my sorrow and joy,
My Beloved, who knowest myself.

My Beloved, who knowest my self.
On the high roof when I churn butter,
When I churn the butter,
My parents rebuke me, thou alone can'st console—
My Beloved, who knowest myself.

They sell good spindles and fine in the market,
They sell in the market,
The eyes of thee too are bewitching,
My Beloved, who knowest myself."

These verses are from a translation in a poem 'Bazar
Vakendian' Rag Pahari, in a Chapter called "Song-Words" of a
Panjabi Singer, in a book about India—*Art and Swadeshi* by A.K.
Coomaraswami. Another poem in the same chapter begins:

"I am mad for my Beloved:
They say, what say they?
Let them say what they will!
Take me for a fool or a madman:
They say, what say they?
Let them say what they will!
I have nothing to do with them,
Whether they be pleased with me or angry,
May One only be gracious to me!
They say, what say they? Let them say what they will!"

As compared with the ancient Indians, the Persians felt the earth
more firmly, as we can see in these verses from their Scripture, the
Zend Avesta, wherein Zarathustra converses with Ahura Mazda.

(From the *Zend Avesta*, translated by James Darmesteter, Clarendon Press, 1895.)

"O Maker of the material world, thou Holy One! Which is the second place where the Earth feels most happy?"

Ahura Mazda answered: "It is the place whereon one of the faithful erects a house with a priest within, with cattle, with a wife, with children, and good herds within; and wherein afterwards the cattle continue to thrive, virtue to thrive, fodder to thrive, the wife to thrive, the child to thrive, the fire to thrive, and every blessing of life to thrive."

"O Maker of the material world, thou Holy One! Which is the third place where the Earth feels most happy?"

Ahura Mazda answered: "It is the place where one of the faithful sows most corn, grass, and fruit, O Zarathustra, where he waters ground that is dry, or drains ground that is too wet."

"O Maker of the material world, thou Holy One! Which is the fourth place where the Earth feels most happy?"

Ahura Mazda answered, "It is the place where there is most increase of flocks and herds."

The Psalms of David, in the Bible, are "sacred songs." In the 19th Psalm we can find the "speech" of God's creation.

"The heavens declare the glory of God; and the firmament showeth his handiwork,

Day unto day uttereth speech, and night unto night showeth knowledge.

There is no speech nor language, where their voice is not heard.

Their line is gone out through all the earth, and their words to the end of the world."

The wise men of Egypt saw the wisdom of the Gods in all of the physical world, as if it were the "writing" of the Gods. In the "Adoration of the Disk" (a hymn to the Sun), King Akhnaten reflects the Egyptian insight as to the relation between heaven and earth. (From Mark Van Doren's *Anthology of World Poetry*.)

Thy dawn, O Ra, opens the new horizon,
And every realm that thou hast made to live
Is conquered by thy love, as Joyous Day
Follows thy footsteps in delightful peace.

Dawn in the East again! The land's awake,
And men leap from their slumber with a song;
They bathe their bodies, clothe them with
     fresh garments,
And lift their hands in happy adoration.

For thou art all that lives, the seed of men,
The son within his mother's womb who knows
The comfort of thy presence near, the babe
To whom thou givest words and growing wisdom;

The chick within the egg, whose breath is thine,
Who runneth from its shell, chirping its joy,
And dancing on its small, unsteady legs
To greet the splendor of the rising sun,

Thy heart created all, this teeming earth,
Its people, herds, creatures that go afoot,
Creatures that fly in air, both land and sea,
Thou didst create them all within thy heart.

And lo, I find thee also in my heart,
I, Khu en Aten, find thee and adore.

To the Greeks the world was bright and beautiful. They too felt the presence of the gods, but as if the gods had died into the earth. So

Orpheus, the Thracian musician who lulled wild beasts and moved trees by his music, sang of Dionysos, the son of Zeus. (From Edouard Schure.)

Zeus is the mighty Demiurgus. Dionysos is his son, his manifested word. Dionysos, glorious spirit, living intelligence, was the splendor of his father's dwelling, One day, as he was bending forward contemplating the abyss of heaven and its constellations, he saw reflected in the azure depths his own image with outstretched arms. Enamoured of this beautiful phantom, his own double, he plunged forward to grasp it. But the image ever escaped him drawing him down to the depths of the abyss. Finally he found himself in a shady, sweet-smelling valley, in full enjoyment of the voluptuous breezes which gently caressed his body. Deep in a grotto he saw Persephone. Maia, the beautiful weaver, was weaving a veil over whose surface could be seen floating the images of all beings. Mute with ravished delight, he stood before the Divine virgin. At this moment the proud Titans and the free Titanides saw him. The former, jealous of his beauty, and the latter, impelled by a mad passion, flung themselves on him like the raging elements, and tore him to pieces.

The thunderbolts of Jupiter destroyed the Titans, and Minerva carried away into the ether the heart of Dionysos: there it became a shining sun. From the smoke of his body have sprung forth the souls of men, ascending again to heaven. When the pale shades have again united into one whole the burning heart of the god, they will arise like flames, and Dionysos in his entirety will spring into ever-renewed life in the heights of the Empyreum.

This is the mystery of the death of Dionysos. Now listen to that of his resurrection. Man are the flesh and blood of Dionysos; the unhappy are his scattered members seeking to be reunited by mutual torture in crime and hatred during thousands of existences. . . . But we, initiates, who know what is above and below, are the saviours of souls. Like magnets we attract them to us, ourselves being attracted by the gods. Thus, by celestial incantations, we reconstitute the living body of the Divinity. . . . In us God dies: in us, also, He returns to birth. (—thus spoke Orpheus.)

The Romans conquered the earth and in so doing lost Heaven! They lost all reverence for the gods, all connection with the spiritual worlds. For them, earthly power meant everything; and one among them, who looked at life, had only the feeling that everything changes and disappears; even man, who, once dead, is no more; that only what man causes is real and when he can no longer see it, it is as if it had never been.

One Roman, Titus Lucretius Carus, wrote the following words. (With regard to this Roman, John Dryden, the English poet, wrote, "He was so much an atheist that he forgot sometimes to be a poet.") The following are excerpts from translations in *The World's Best Poems*, Van Doren & Lapolla.

No Single Thing Abides

No single thing abides; but all things flow.
Fragment to fragment clings—the things thus grow
  Until we know and name them. By degrees
They melt, and are no more the things we know.

Nothing abides. Thy seas (O earth) in delicate haze
Go off; those mooned sands forsake their place;
  And where they are, shall other seas in turn
Mow with their scythes of whiteness other bays.

Lo, how the terraced towers, and monstrous round,
Of league-long ramparts rise from out the ground,
  With gardens in the clouds. Then all is gone,
And Babylon is a memory and a mound.

Found, angular, soft, brittle, dry, cold, warm,
Things *are* their qualities: things *are* their form—
  And these in combination, even as bees,
Not singly but combined, make up the swarm:

And when the qualities like bees on wing,
Having a moment clustered, cease to cling,
  As the thing dies without its qualities,
So die the qualities without the thing.
The seeds that once were we take flight and fly,

Winnowed to earth, or whirled along the sky,
Not lost but disunited. Life lives on.
It is the lives, the lives, the lives, that die,

—Titus Lucretius Carus, 95–52 B.C.

From *Against the Fear of Death*, Another poem by the same Roman includes these lines:

What has this bugbear Death to frighten man,
If souls can die, as well as bodies can?

From sense of grief and pain we shall be free;
We shall not feel, because we shall not be.

It was in this Roman time that Jesus Christ lived on earth. In a faraway little colony of Rome, he brought new words to men on earth when he said, "I am in the Father, and ye in me, and I in you. The words that I speak unto you I speak not of myself, but the Father that dwelleth in me, he doeth the works."

"The Kingdom of God cometh not with observation. Neither shall they say, Lo here! Lo there! for behold the Kingdom of God is within you."

And it was Christ who, before his death, said, "Yet a little while and the world seeth me no more; but ye see me: because I live ye shall live also."

Many centuries have run their course since the men of ancient India sought to unite themselves with God, the "Beloved." Mankind has all but forsaken its devotion to the creative Word, the wisdom of life. Once more, however, a word is given—a message, "The *words* that I speak unto you I speak not of myself, but the Father that dwelleth in me, he doeth the *works*."

And Lucretius receives an answer—"because I live ye shall live also."

Runes and Rags

One form of ancient musical speech was the "rag" (pronounced rahg) of India. In olden times these rags were very sacred; one could not sing them just any time. They belonged to certain seasons, times, events or purposes. Each one had its own use. They were said to be as powerful as the music of Orpheus, for they could affect the elements, could make flames of fire appear, could bring rain, and so on. As "song-words" they had power to make, to move, to form, and shape. (We know something of this ourselves, though in a different way. Harsh words kill something in us. Ugly words do the same. Kindly or beautiful words can move us to worthwhile actions.) In the rag the tune had as much meaning as the words. There were even wordless rags. Rags were sung to invoke help from the gods, to charm houses against evil spirits and demons.. The following was a charm against coughing:

A quotation in *Indian Myth and Legend*

"As the soul with the soul's desires swiftly to a
      distance flies,
Thus do thou, O cough, fly forth along the soul's
      course of flight.
As a well-sharpened arrow swiftly to a distance flies,
      Thus do thou, O cough, fly forth along the expanse
            of the earth.
As the rays of the sun swiftly to a distance fly,
      Thus do thou, O cough, fly forth along the flood
            of the sea."

—D. A. MacKenzie

And the following is an invocation to the gods in *Indian Myth and Legend*

"From the sins which knowingly or unknowingly we have committed, do ye, all gods, of one accord release us.

If awake or asleep, to sin inclined, I have committed a sin, may what has been, and what shall be, as if from a wooden post, release me."

—D. A. MacKenzie

The Norse runes were also magical. *Rune* means 'secret.' A tune was a mysterious song, a mysterious speech, and a mysterious writing. The ancestors of the Norsemen had an alphabet called runes. These were sounds that had great power and had been given to men by Odin, the King of the Gods. He made characters of these runes and they were risted (written) on many different substances, then scattered all over the world so that men might find them and gain wisdom from Odin.

In R. B. Anderson's *Norse Mythology*, page 260, we read:

"Odin's runes represent the might and wisdom with which he rules all nature. . . . Odin, as master of runes, is the spirit that subdues and controls physical nature. He governs inanimate nature, the wind, the sea, the fire, and the mind of man, the hate of the enemy, and the love of woman. Everything submits to his mighty sway, and thus the runes were risted on all possible things in heaven and on earth. He is the spirit of the world, that pervades everything, the almighty Creator, father of gods and men."

Further, the story of how Odin won his knowledge of nature is explained.

"Odin hung nine days on the Tree Yggdrasil and sacrificed himself to himself, wounded himself with his own spear. Odin had given his eye in pawn for a drink from Mimer's fountain. The spear with which he now wounds himself shows how solemnly he consecrates himself. For the sake of this struggle to acquire knowledge, the spirit offers itself to itself. It knows what hardships and sufferings must be encountered on the road to knowledge, but it bravely faces these obstacles, it wants to wrestle with them. Nine nights Odin hangs on the tree. (Rome was not built in a day.) He fasts. You must also curb your bodily appetites and, like Odin, look down into the depths and penetrate the mysteries of nature with your mind. Then you will learn all those wonderful songs that Odin learned crying before he fell from the Tree.

Odin is the author of the runic incantations that played so conspicuous a part in the social and religious life of the Norseman."

In the following verses, we will hear how Odin won the knowledge of the runes which were to help mankind.

from *Odin's Song in the Edda*

I know that I hung
On a wind—rocked tree
Nine whole nights—

With a spear wounded
And to Odin offered,
Myself to myself;

Bread no one gave me,
Nor a horn of drink,
Downward I peered,
To runes applied myself,
Wailing I learned them,
Then fell down hence.

Then I began to bear fruit
And to know many things.

Word by word
I sought out words,
Fact by fact
I sought out facts.

Runes thou wilt find,
And explained characters,
Very large characters,
Very potent characters.

The runes are then described, and here are some of them:

Help the first is called,
For that will help thee
Against strifes and cares.   *the first rune*

If men place
Bonds on my limbs,
I so sing
That I can walk:
The fetter starts from my feet
And the manacle from my hands.   *the fourth rune*

I see a shot from a hostile hand,
A shaft flying amid the host,
So swift it cannot fly,
That I cannot arrest it.   *the fifth rune*

If one wounds me
Also if a man
Declares hatred to me,
Harm shall consume them sooner than me.   *the sixth rune*

Where hatred grows
Among the sons of men
That I can quickly assuage.   *the eighth rune*

If I stand in need
My bark on the water to save,
I can the wind
On the waves allay,
And the sea lull.   *the ninth rune*

If I have to lead
My ancient friends to battle,
Under their shields I sing,
And with power they go
Safe to the fight,
Safe from the fight,
Safe on every side they go.   *the eleventh rune*

There are eighteen runes in this Song of Odin.

Sound and Meaning in Words

In our day there are learned people who work so hard to find and use words that express just the right meaning that they deaden the words. Those who read what they write have a hard time understanding what they mean. For instance:

> The major part of teaching effort in the primary grades, and frequently in the intermediate grades, is directed toward teaching pupils how to acquire or improve their ability to read the materials of their respective grades. Stress is placed on accuracy of comprehension and on such basic skills as word recognition, word meaning and sentence understanding which are necessary in comprehension. The importance attached to acquiring and extending these abilities in reading is sound: a reader obviously must be able to get the author's ideas from the printed page. (This was written by a teacher's college professor. Can you tell me, without our reading it again, exactly what the writer's ideas are?)

Now I would like to read you something from *The Oregon Trail*:

> "The air grew fresh and cool, the distant mountains frowned more gloomily; there was a low muttering of thunder, and dense black masses of cloud rose heavily behind the broken peaks. At first they were fringed with silver by the afternoon sun; but soon thick blackness overspread the sky, and the

desert around us was wrapped in gloom. There was an awful sublimity in the hoarse murmuring of the thunder and the somber shadows that involved the mountains and the plain. The storm broke with a zig-zag blinding flash, a terrific crash of thunder and a hurricane that howled over the prairie dashing floods of water against us."

What is the difference between this paragraph and the first one? What is it in the second that helps to give us almost the same experience as the writer had? The *sounds* in the words! They bring the words to life. We breathe the 'fresh cool air' and feel it on our cheeks and hands. We hear the very sound of the thunder in the words, "a low muttering of thunder." "The hoarse murmuring of the thunder," "a terrific crash of thunder." The sounds of the words help us feel the coloring of the air, the earth and sky: "dense black masses of cloud," "thick blackness," "gloom," "somber shadows." We blink in the sounds of the words, "zig-zag blinding flash." We hear the wind in "hurricane," "howled," and the water in "dashing floods of water against us." We see the sharp outline of the mountain in "broken peaks," the shining edges of the clouds in "fringed with silver by the afternoon sun."

These words have life because they are sounding something out. Their meaning can be heard in their sounds.

Can you think of words that sound like what they mean?

tap, drip, roll, wiggle, tickle, twitch, whirl, whir, whistle, whisper, rustle, bustle, squeak, chatter, roar, breathe, choke, strangle, dangle, bellow, shout, dark, star, crackle, wrinkle, splash, squash, hollow . . .

Now we come to the question of why it is that we can understand sounds in speech, and why it is that such speech is more alive for us than that which is less musical. When we study sounds in words, we really find two kinds of sounds: the vowel sounds and the consonants. If we can find out what lives in the vowel sounds and the consonant sounds, then we will learn a secret of sound in speech.

The Vowels

We often use the vowels alone, to express something. What do these sounds tell us?

Oh! Ah! Oo! Ee! Aye! Hey! Ugh! Aw! Eh! Ow!

They express feelings that live in our souls, and when these sounds enter words, they bring into the words just those human feelings that live in the sounds, as in

hope, star, gloom, seek, stay, ugly, awful, ever, shout

The Consonants

The consonants, in general, cannot stand alone. They are always longing for union with a vowel. Alone they can only whisper. Together with vowels they can be heard. But they have the power of shaping the vowel sounds, so that words with the same vowel sounds, but different consonants, give us different pictures:

star, dark, hark, hard, tart, father

or

crash, flash, lash, smash, thrash

or

sleep, peep, creep, meet, sweet, fleet, greet

Eurythmy helps us to understand the vowels and the consonants, for in eurythmy the sounds become gestures:

c̲rash, f̲lash, l̲ash, sm̲ash, har̲k, har̲d

If you will do the eurythmy gestures for the consonants I have underlined, you will experience differences in these sounds in the right way.

The consonants carry the vowels, and the vowels fill them just as tones fill the shape of a flute or a violin or a trumpet. And just as each shape of instrument makes the same tone sound different, the consonants lend their shaping power to the sound of the vowel. The vowels are the tones. The consonants are the instruments on which the tones are played.

Moreover, the consonants are formed through the shape of the human body. Different parts of the body can be heard in the consonants: the lips, the teeth, the tongue, the throat.

All the consonants contained in any language are actually variations of 12 original consonants. (In our English alphabet we have 21 consonants. In the Finnish language there are only 12 consonants.) In the chart below, we will write the original consonants in capital letters, and the variations in small letters.

1. B)
2. M) . . . . .Lip sounds
   p)

3. F)
   v) . . . . .Upper teeth, under lip

4. S)
   z) . . . . .Teeth
   c) (soft)

5. N)
6. D) . . . . .Tongue tip
7. T)
8. L)

9. G)
   k) . . . . .Tongue root
   q)
   c) (hard)

10. H) . . . . .A consonant that is out in the air, consonantic
                     handling of air.

11. R) . . . . .Sides of tongue

12. CH) …………Top of tongue and roof of mouth

j)

w) …………..Consonant changes into a vowel

We said before that the consonants cannot stand alone; they can only whisper and become filled with sound as soon as they unite with a vowel. Compare:

h-p with hope, g-l-m with gloom, s-t-r- with star, s-p-k with speak

While the vowels express our inner feelings, the consonants express something that lives in outer nature.

- In the sound of F we experience fire, flame, flash.
- In H we experience the air, in words like hover, hear, and heaven.
- In L we experience the watery element in such words as liquid, lake, leak, flowing, limpid.
- In the sound of G we feel the element of earth in the words: Ground, dig, grave, grind,

So it is that the consonants bear in them the shaping power that works in nature. The vowels reveal our human feelings. In the consonants and vowels together, or in the spoken word, we unite with the world around us.

The Parts of Speech

(These thoughts can be brought to a class as it takes up a review of the parts of speech.)

We often hear it said that animals do everything but talk. We observe that animals communicate their feelings. They show what they want by running back and forth, by barking, bleating, calling, and any number of other such actions, But they cannot shape words. The parrots and minahs, of course, imitate human speech, but they also imitate other birds and animal noises.

Let us try to think of the ways of life in the animal realm. Animals live in movement, in affection, in protection of their young, in hunting and eating, in relationships with the seasons. The beaver, the spider, the ant and the bee are all workers. Young animals play and cavort. In all their ways of life, however, one thing is missing: SPEECH! The power of speech lies in the human realm. In it we can find a key to the differences between animals and human beings.

Suppose animals *could* shape words in relation to what they are able to do and to feel; what kinds of words could they use? They might be able to use:

Verbs	Adjectives	Adverbs
run	pleasant	swiftly
creep	tasty	loudly
pounce	dangerous	stealthily
crouch	exciting	hungrily
gnaw	comfortable	silently
scratch	gay	busily
dig	hungry	slowly
fly	brave	craftily

Could they use *nouns*? Have they that, in their natures, which would enable them to use nouns, to name things? Dogs, which are the animals closest to human beings, do know one person from another, do know their own names, and may even prick up their ears when their master's names are spoken. Dogs are, in general, the most humanized of animals. But dogs cannot utter a name.

The human being can speak his own name and the names of all creatures and things. The Bible tells us how Adam named all creatures after God created them.

When we name someone or something, we are using a consciousness which the animals do not have. We are aware of what the name means, of what lies behind it. As soon as we know what something is, or what it does, we find a name for it, and that name, ever after informs us of all that it means.

lion	angel	stone	tinker	rich man
cow	devil	plant	tailor	poor man
mouse	rascal	animal	soldier	beggar man
frog	saint	man	sailor	thief

How differently we deal with each of these!

Like the animals we *act*—   and in our speech there
are action words: **Verbs**.

feel—   **Adjectives**

*act in
various ways*—   **Adverbs**

But, unlike the animals,
we *think* and *know*—   **Nouns**

The four main parts of speech seem to rise out of the nature of living beings, but only the human being can actually speak and use them all. He has the power that lies behind the noun: to perceive and name and think about everything in the world.

Perhaps if the animal had this power (of the noun), it would be able to speak; but even its actions show that it lacks this power. The animal expresses itself through bodily movements and bodily noises that are monotonously the same. The animal's voice is truly pitiful, like that of a dumb, or mute, man who struggles to talk and sounds like an animal. If we think about the four main parts of speech, we can see that the noun, the name, represents knowledge, and knowledge is a human faculty. We can think of the people of India who, even today, believe that by uttering, and thus thinking on, the most sacred *name* in the universe—"OM," they will gain the wisdom of the world and of the heavens so as to understand God's will.

In all languages, whether it be French, German, Dutch, Russian, or English, we have nouns, verbs, adjectives, and adverbs, because they express the full human being, whether he be a Frenchman, a German, a Dutchman, a Russian, or an American.

A Concluding Chapter for a Grammar Notebook

(This can be used as the basis for a class discussion and a notebook dictation.)

The study of grammar is like a journey through a wonderfully designed building. One cannot compare this building with the steel-framed skyscrapers of New York. Although its structure is just as firm, it is shaped as if it were in movement. Or we can imagine a building that has been sculptured rather than erected brick by brick. There are always human beings living in it, giving it its shape through their own feelings, thoughts, and deeds. They are its sculptors. And as we explore this building of the human language we discover it to be an image of human nature.

In our study of the sounds in speech we discovered that the vowels and consonants arise from the very nature of the human being and his perceptions of the world. Then we explored words as parts of speech and found that the nouns, verbs, and adjectives spring from our thoughts, deeds and feelings. We realized that through the nine parts of speech we can give a complete picture of a thought or a mood or an event.

When we grouped the parts of speech in clauses and phrases, we were able to enclose one thought in another; to join, relate and separate various thoughts. By learning the parts of the sentence, we found thoughts and memories and ideas can be expressed in an orderly, complete, and understandable way.

Last of all, we have seen how the parts of speech change their form when it is necessary. The verb can express six kinds of time; it can be active or passive; it can even act like a noun or an adjective. So, too, the nouns and pronouns fit themselves into the meaning of the language in various ways, by changing their case, their number, their person. Adjectives and adverbs can stretch themselves to express more or less of the degree in which something may be so. In these changing forms the design of the language becomes ever more active.

When, through our understanding of grammar, we see the wondrous building of our language, we grow in the clarity of our own power of thinking.

Mrs. Grammar's Ball

from *Great Grandmother's Piece Book*

Mrs. Grammar once gave a fine ball
To the nine different parts of our speech
    To the short and the tall,
    To the stout and the small,
There were pies, plums, and puddings for each.

    And first little Articles came
    In a hurry to make themselves known;
        Fat A, AN and THE—
        But none of the three
    Could stand for a minute alone.

Then Adjectives came to announce
That their dear friends the Nouns were at hand;
    Rough, rougher, and roughest,
    Tough, tougher, and toughest,
Fat, merry, good-natured, and grand.

    The Nouns were indeed on their way,
    Tens of thousands and more, I should think;
        For each name that we utter,
        Shop, shoulder, or shutter—
    Is a Noun; lion, lady, or link.

The Pronouns were hastening fast
To push the nouns out of their places:
    I, thou, he, and she,
    You, it, they, and we,
With their sprightly, intelligent faces.

    Someone cried, "Make way for the Verbs!
    A great crowd is coming to view."
        To light and to smite,
        To fight and to bite,
        To be and to have and to do.

The Adverbs attend on the Verbs.
Behind, as their footmen, they run;
As thus, "To fight badly"
    And "Run away gladly"
Show how running and fighting were done.

      Prepositions came, in, by and near,
      With conjunctions, a wee little band,
        As either you or he
        But neither I nor she,
      They held their great friends by the hand.

Then, too, with a Hip! Hip! Hoorah!
Rushed in Interjections uproarious.
    Dear me! Well-a-day!
    When they saw the display,
"Ha! Ha!" they all shouted out, "Glorious!"

      But alas what misfortunes were nigh!
      While the fun and the feasting pleased each,
        Pounced on them at once
        A monster—a Dunce!
      And confounded the nine parts of speech.

Help Friends, to the rescue! On you
For aid Verb and Article call.
    O give your protection
    To poor interjection,
Noun, Pronoun, Conjunction and all.

Speech Exercises

For Grade 1

I am the giant!
When I mumble and grumble
The whole earth doth rumble.

I am the witch!
I spit and I spat
With my skinny black cat.

I am the King!
I hold in my hand
The laws of the land.

I am the knight!
I fight the King's foe
With battle-ax and bow.

I am the gnome!
I dig in the ground
That gold may be found.

I am the Queen!
In my silvery gown
And shining crown.

I am the Lady!
I primp and I preen
And I follow the Queen.

I am the fairy!
I fly in the air
And live everywhere.

I am the elf!
Here I whisper and peep,
There I flip, skip, and leap.

For Grades 1 through 4

This collection includes excerpts from poets as well as verses contrived for special needs in the class.

Round the rough and rugged rock, the ragged rascal ran.

Theophilus Thistle, the unsuccessful thistle sifter, thrust three thousand thistles through the thick of his thumb.

Peter Piper picked a peck of pickled peppers,
A peck of pickled peppers Peter Piper picked.
If Peter Piper picked a peck of pickled peppers,
Where's the peck of pickled peppers Peter Piper picked?

How much wood would a woodchuck chuck,
If a woodchuck could chuck wood?
A woodchuck would chuck all the wood he could chuck,
If a woodchuck could chuck wood.

The owl and the eel and the warming pan
Went to call on the soap-fat man.
The soap-fat man, he was not within:
He'd gone for a ride on his rolling pin.
So they all came back by way of the town
And turned the meeting house upside down.

—Laura E. Richards

A BRA CA DA BRA
BRA DA CA RA BA
CA DA RA BRA BA (fast on the last line)

Did he shut the lid, the lid that was locked?
If he did, it didn't stay shut.

The waves washed the caves,
Rolled into the caves,
The mountainous waves
Filled the wide-sea caves.

Little Miss Munching Mouse
Munches mince-meat in my house,
Lamp or light no longer lit,
Biting, nibbling, bit by bit,
Bits of bread, of beans, of buns,
Comes the cat to catch—the crumbs!

Fly pretty butterfly!
Bumble-bee fly.
Flash proud beetle,
Beside the pale flower.

Nid nod Nanny goat,
Nibble Nellie's petticoat
Never nip nettles,
Nor lip daisy petals.

Hark, hark the gong!
Heavy clangs the gong,
Ding—dang—dong,
Hurry, hurry home,
Going, going, gone.

Trip, trip, trill,
My lady's lost her frill,
The fairies found it
In the frost,
Trip, trip, trill.

Far sails the sailor,
Green sweeps the sea,
While the waves wash over the yellow sand,
And dragons are dancing in dragon-land
To a musical tune by the light of the moon
Who shines in a moon-horn tree.

She sells sea-shells by the sea shore;
The shells she sells are sea-shells I'm sure.

A tutor that tooted the flute
Tried to tutor two tooters to toot.
Said the two to the tutor,
"Is it harder to toot, or
To tutor two tooters to toot?"

Betty Botta bought some butter.
"But," she said, "This butter's bitter.
If I put it in my batter
It will make my batter bitter.
But a bit of better butter
Will make my bitter batter better."

So she bought a bit of butter
Better than the bitter butter,
And it made her bitter batter better.
So 'twas better Betty Botta
Bought a bit of better butter.

Grades 5 through 8

Gold! Gold! Gold! Gold!
Bright and yellow, hard and cold!
Molten, graven, hammered and rolled,
Heavy to get and light to hold,
Hoarded, bartered, bought and sold,
Stolen, borrowed, squandered, doled,
Spurned by the young, but hugged by the old
To the very verge of the churchyard mold.
Amidst the mists and coldest frosts,
With stoutest wrists and loudest boasts,
He thrusts his fists against the posts
And still insists he sees the ghosts.

Moon on the field and the foam,
Moon on the mount and the world,
Moon, bring him home! bring him home!
Safe from the dark and the cold,
Home, sweet moon, bring him home,
Home with the flock to the fold.

And the muttering grew to a grumbling,
And the grumbling grew to a mighty rumbling,
And out of the houses the rats came tumbling.

—Pied Piper

The curfew tolls the knell of parting day;
The lowing herd winds slowly o'er the lea;
The plowman homeward plows his weary way
      And leaves the world to darkness and to me.

—Thomas Gray (Elegy)

We are stars that sing,
We sing with our light,
We are the birds of fire,
We fly across the heavens,
Our light is a star.
  —Red Indian lyric

Rumble, blunder, stumble, thunder,
Wrangle, tangle, jingle-jangle,
Fluttery, stuttery, bog, fog,
  Missing his tack,
  Changing his track,
  Losing his threads,
  Mixing his "heads,"
Flash! Dash! Splash! Crash!
Slowly, fastly, grimly, ghastly,
Firstly, secondly, thirdly, lastly.
  —W. S. Gilbert

Never more;
Miranda,
Never more;
Only the high peaks hoar;
And Aragon a torrent at the door.
No sound
In the walls of the halls where falls
The tread
Of the feet of the dead to the ground.
No sound.
Only the boom
Of the far waterfall like Doom.
  —Hillaire Belloc

Make thyself flutt'ring wings of thy fast flying thought
And fly forth to thy love whosoever she be.
Oh fly forth to thy love with thy fast-flying thought,
Whosoever she be, on thy fluttering wings.

—Spenser

When a twister, a-twisting, will twist him a twist;
For the twisting of his twist, he three times doth intwist;
But if one of the twines of the twist do untwist,
The twine that untwisteth, untwisteth the twist.

Untwining the twine that untwisteth between,
He twirls, with the twister, the two in a twine.
Then twice having twisted the twines of the twine,
He twisteth the twine he had twined in twain.

The twain that, in twining, before in the twine,
As twines were intwisted; he now doth untwine:
Twixt the twain intertwisting a twine more between,
He, twirling his twister, makes a twist of the twine.

One old Oxford ox opening oysters;
Two tee-totums totally tired of trying to trot to Tedsbury;
Three thick thumping tigers tickling trout;
Four fat friars fanning fainting flies;
Five frippy Frenchmen foolishly fishing for flies;
Six sportsmen shooting snipes;
Seven Severn salmons swallowing shrimps;
Eight Englishmen eagerly examining Europe;
Nine nimble noblemen nibbling nonpareils;
Ten tinker stinkling upon ten tin tinder boxes
       with ten tenpenny tacks;
Eleven elephants elegantly equipped;
Twelve typographical topographers typically translating types.

For a child with a nasal voice

Tell me truly the tale of the town—
How Dolly Toley tumbled down
With a flour bag full of fine white flour,
Dusting the doorstep, spilling a shower
Of thick white dust
That dimmed the sun and covered the moon with crust.

For a child with heavy speech

Flip, flap, flip, flap—
Horse in saddle—
Strip, strap! whip, whap!
Flip, strip, whip—
Flap, strap, whap—
Flip the whip, flap the strap,
Whap!

To soften a strident voice

Now the cloud
Sounds aloud,
Hums a tune
Around the moon.
Hear the sound
Howling 'round.
Who is where
In that high air?
Airy cloud,
You are loud!

For "embodiment" in consonants

In grinding ground
My grist I found.
Cracking the clod
I clove the sod.
Digging, jigging,
I dug the junk.
Algebra!

For mobility of speech

Rivers and seas, seas and rivers—
Rivers and seas and rills—
Rills and seas and rivers—
Rivers and seas and rills and ripples—

Ripples and rills and seas and rivers—
Rivers and seas and rills and ripples rolling—
Rolling ripples and rills and seas and rivers—
Rivers and seas and rills and ripples rolling and rilling—
Rilling and rolling ripples and rills and seas and rivers.

These final three exercises are not prescriptions. They represent attempts to meet needs of various children.

To help correct hurried, breathless speech

Slow, slow,   (very slowly, on the breath)
Go so slow,
Over and over,
Over and over.
Oh, Ah, Ah, Oh
Slow to come, slow to go.
Open and close,
Open, close,
Out and in,
Thick, thin

Never let a butterfly (fast)
Travel in a tin.
Catch it in a bottle top.
Hold it in a rain drop.
Keep it in.

To strengthen a child with scattered tendencies

Bring the blossom.
Bless the bloom.
Begin the blessing.
Bestow the boon.

To help a tense child

The lovely lily lifts her head,
Looking aloft the live-long day,
Blessed by the loving light of the sun.

Three little thimbles
Tripped through the thread,
Took a tuck,
Tied a tack,
Did a trick
To take them back
To trip through the thread
To three little thimbles.

Faster than express trains,
Quicker than a wink,
Flitting little humming bird
Sips a honey drink.
Whist, whiz, dip, sip
From a flower's petal-lip.

The snail is slow.
See it go
Over the stone,
Oh so slow
All alone,
Over and over
Stone after stone.